MEET THE CANDIDATES 2020

BERNIE SANDERS

A VOTER'S GUIDE

Series Edited by
SCOTT DWORKIN

Compiled and Written by Grant Stern

Skyhorse Publishing

Skyhorse Publishing books may be purchased in bulk at special discounts for
sales promotion, corporate gifts, fund-raising, or educational purposes. Special
editions can also be created to specifications. For details, contact the Special
Sales Department, Skyhorse Publishing, 307 West 36th Street, 11th Floor,
New York, NY 10018 or info@skyhorsepublishing.com.

Skyhorse® and Skyhorse Publishing® are registered trademarks of Skyhorse
Publishing, Inc.®, a Delaware corporation.

Visit our website at www.skyhorsepublishing.com.

10 9 8 7 6 5 4 3 2 1

Library of Congress Cataloging-in-Publication Data is available on file.

Cover design by Brian Peterson
Cover photo credit: Mark Makela/Getty Images

ISBN: 978-1-5107-5025-8
Ebook ISBN: 978-1-5107-5033-3

Printed in the United States of America

CONTENTS

INTRODUCTION TO BERNIE SANDERS

BY SERIES EDITOR SCOTT DWORKIN

I had the opportunity to meet Senator Bernie Sanders in early 2012 while I was a senior adviser to the Congressional Progressive Caucus's (CPC) nonprofit foundation focused on political coalition building and fund-raising. In our short encounter, I learned a lot about him. I could tell he was extremely passionate and a very forceful messenger for the progressive cause.

What was clear to me then, as is it is now, is that Senator Sanders was willing to do the hard work—not just campaign events and rallies, but to sit down, roll his sleeves up, and talk about how we could make big changes in Washington.

Sanders was the only senator we had in the CPC. He was also one of the most active electeds overall in the entire CPC, which makes sense since he was a cofounder of the caucus and its first chairman.[1] Sanders and his staff were involved in most of the retreats we hosted for progressives, and they would take the time to join in on organizing calls and other events.

Sanders knew exactly what he stood for, as most people probably do now. You knew exactly where he was on any issue, even if it wasn't popular at the time. If it's the right thing to do, he doesn't mind standing out in front and taking the flak for doing what he believes is right. He doesn't tiptoe around anything. One of the things that Bernie Sanders does really well is connect with people who welcome his blunt honesty in a world of politicians filled with so many liars. The senator can get to a simple bottom line quickly and spell out what he stands for clearly and concisely.

He's spent decades helping tilt Congress more left, pushing the Democratic Party to move back toward the New Deal politics that gave them control of the federal government for forty years that coincided with a tremendous economic boom. He is a real leader and durable supporter of progressive ideals.

Something I found truly refreshing was the fact that Sanders wasn't worried about his campaign fund-raising—not that he needed to be, since he represented a state where President Obama won by thirty-seven points in 2008.[2] What he was really worried about was what Democrats could do to get more organized and win elections, how Democrats could coordinate better, and how they could get on the same page at every level—and especially about how members of the left wing of the party would communicate with each other.

And for the twenty-eight years he's been in Congress, Sanders hasn't really been a person that money could influence, something that really sets him apart from the rest of the presidential nominees.

One of the reasons he is able to not worry about fund-raising is because his grassroots fund-raising is so strong. He's not constantly worried about pleasing rich donors as other 2020 presidential candidates might be, excluding Senator Warren, who has sworn them off entirely. Bernie Sanders is not afraid to take on the rampant corruption in Washington or fight back against big banks and Wall Street. That's because Sanders cares more about the American people than he does about corporations. He isn't up to his neck in contributions from hedge fund managers, stockbrokers, and fat-cat bankers.

He owes them nothing.

Sanders has successfully helped pushed for a more progressive Congress, Democratic Party, and America since 1990, with lots of help from his wife Jane. The end result, nearly three decades later, is that the CPC he founded has had a key role in cementing the speakership for then-Minority Leader Nancy Pelosi, who in turn gave its members more committee appointments and new funding to expand their House Democratic Policy and Communications Committee.[3]

"All the challenges to Leader Pelosi are coming from her right, in an apparent effort to make the party even more conservative and bent toward corporate interests. Hard pass," tweeted Representative-elect Alexandria Ocasio-Cortez (D-NY) in November 2018 (she is a leading new member of the Congressional Progressive Caucus today). "So long as Leader Pelosi remains the most progressive candidate for Speaker, she can count on my support."[4]

When you hear about the new representatives that make up the CPC today, who hold the "radical" sort of new progressive ideas, a lot of that came from Sanders. And if you think they seem radical now, imagine how he sounded when he was talking about those progressive policies almost thirty years ago. Sanders even embraced the fact that his ideas were radical, as he said in this 1988 C-SPAN interview, when responding to the question of what kind of president he would like to see in the White House:

> *I would like to see somebody who has the guts to begin to stand up to the people who own this country. To recognize in our nation today we have an extreme disparity between the rich and the poor. That elections are bought and sold and controlled by people who have huge sums of money. So my first concern, is to have a president who has the courage to look reality in the face and say that we need some radical changes in this country.*[5]

His radical ideas for the left have been proven to be more popular in the United States than almost any part of the Republican Party's agenda.[6]

One of the things that Sanders has really pushed hard for over the years, along with a more progressive Congress, is for a structural overhaul of our health care system into a single-payer national health insurance system. He's always worked to make universal health care a right for all in America.

Obamacare didn't go as far as Sanders wanted it to go. Yet, the Affordable Care Act (ACA) still touched on a significant priority in his national agenda by vastly expanding America's system of community health centers, which also provide dental services to one in thirteen people.[7] The Vermont senator's contribution to the ACA led to what has to be the greatest expansion of community health centers since they were created in the 1960s during President Lyndon B. Johnson's War on Poverty.

Beginning all the way back in 1991, Sanders supported Secretary Hillary Clinton's attempt to fix America's broken health care system. Sanders expanded on his thoughts about health care in a C-SPAN interview:

> *We are spending more than any other country on earth and yet we're getting very little out of it. Clearly I think the solution must be a movement toward a single-payer universal comprehensive healthcare, similar to what exists in Canada. People say that the Canadian system has problems, it does. But if we understand they are spending 40 percent less per capita than we are, I think by level funding healthcare at the present level of $756 billion we can eliminate virtually all of those problems. And have the best healthcare system in the world where every man, woman and child, has all of the healthcare that they need, without any out of pocket expense.*[8]

Ironically, his support for Clinton became a major campaign issue in the 2016 Democratic primary. Just after the second-to-last debate of that election, she rhetorically asked where Sanders was while she was pushing for universal health coverage in 1993 at a campaign event in St. Louis. The Sanders campaign quickly tweeted out a photo of then-Representative Sanders literally right behind First Lady Clinton, and the Senator later tweeted a handwritten photo of the two of them with her thanks for his support.[9,10]

By 2016, Clinton had abandoned the plan for a single-payer health insurance option and fiercely attacked Sanders for advocating it, but it was essentially the same plan that he worked to pass starting in 1993 when he filed the "Health Care as a Right for All" bill, which she also discarded back then.[11]

It's always hard to find out what someone actually stands for, but I think one of the greatest things that Sanders has going for him is his penchant to be brutally honest and blunt—something a lot of Americans appreciate. His loud and clear voice during Senate hearings is exactly what some of the most corrupt people on earth need to hear. One example of Sanders being blunt in a Committee hearing is his questioning of Acting Environmental Protection Agency Administrator Andrew Wheeler, where he said:

> *I found it interesting Mr. Wheeler, you are the nominee to be head of the Environmental Protection Agency and you just, in your opening statement did not mention the word climate change. Now how does that happen that a nominee to be the head of the Environmental Protection Agency does not mention the words climate change at a time where the scientific community thinks that climate change is the great environmental crisis facing this planet.*[12]

Or when Sanders confronted secretary of education nominee Betsy DeVos during her confirmation hearing:

> *Mrs. DeVos, there is a growing fear I think in this country that we are moving toward what some would call an*

oligarchic form of society. Where a small number of very, very wealthy billionaires control, to a significant degree, our economic and political life. Would you be so kind as to tell us how much money your family has contributed to the Republican Party over the years? [. . .] have heard the number was 200 million. Does that sound in the ballpark? [. . .] My question is, and I don't mean to be rude, but do you think, if you were not a multi-billionaire, if your family had not made hundreds of millions of dollars of contributions to the Republican Party, that you would be sitting here today?[13]

That is brutal. Not many senators would have the courage to question a billionaire like that. But again, this is where Sanders's immunity to being bought with contributions is helpful.

He is not the kind of person to walk away and back off from a fight. He confronts bullies. That makes Sanders a really strong candidate. An anecdote from the *New Republic* back in 1983 perfectly encapsulates Sanders's political temperament:[14]

"Bernie's a pretty good Mayor," said one resident. "But he's a real confrontationist, and that's going to catch up with him one day." To which Sanders replies, "to be cooperative means to be co-opted. If I don't do anything, what the hell was I elected for?"

This is why Sanders is so beloved by his supporters. He stands firmly with the American people against a small group of special interests and billionaires dominating our politics. He's what we could consider to be the opposite of Donald Trump—what Trump would be if he were liberal, had morals, and actually cared about the American people.

In addition to him being able to stand up to Trump in person, Sanders has enough social reach where he can forcefully push back. Last year, Sanders reached millions of viewers with his own town hall events, through what the *New Yorker* described as a budding "digital media empire."[15] Democrats need someone like Sanders who can respond both swiftly and sternly to Republicans, especially through social media platforms.

I'm not sure if Sanders can definitely beat Trump; the early polling says no. But if you could imagine Sanders in a debate with Trump, you know that Sanders is not going to let Trump just talk over him.

Sanders would definitely stand up to Trump. Without a doubt.

Sanders does have several weaknesses. Expect to see those trotted out early in the primary, especially since Hillary Clinton never really focused the 2016 contest on opposition research.

One major challenge is the fact that there are a lot of Hillary supporters who still don't generally like him. A former Clinton staffer recently said: "I think we are all just scarred by 2016 at large and would like to prevent that again."[16] But some Clinton staffers have even started a full-fledged anti-Sanders campaign in 2018, with the hope he is forced out of the running. The bottom line is, it was a tough primary battle in 2016, and some people will never get over that, no matter what Sanders says or does.

Another Sanders weakness is that he's not a long-term member of the Democratic Party, and that's going to pose a serious problem with some primary voters. They want a person who's committed to the party and will back up the party and support the party. Not someone who's half in and half out, not in it by name but wants all the support from the same people. It's going to be a big issue.

Some more baggage for Sanders includes him being used by foreign adversaries like Russia to divide the Democratic Party.[17] This, along with his campaign's links to convicted former Trump campaign chairman Paul Manafort via former Sanders campaign manager Tad Devine, poses major problems for the campaign.[18]

A huge weakness I see for Sanders right now is the fact that he's a self-promoting "democratic socialist," especially since the term "socialist" is not very popular right now. The level of negative sentiment around the word "socialist" doesn't seem like it's going to change, as it's remained the same for the last nine years.[19] Plus, Trump has now weaponized the word "socialism" against all Democrats, along with his friends at Fox News.[20] "Socialist" will be the catchphrase that Trump likely uses to attack any Democrat, but it seems like it would be most effective against Sanders. I can see Trump using it over and over again, beating it into the ground. Even more troublesome, I can see that potentially working. That poses a big risk for the Democrats, especially in every swing state.

The word "socialism" still has a lot of negative connotations attached to it, even though the kind of socialism they are describing is not actually the kind of socialism Sanders is advocating for. What Trump is describing as socialism—state ownership of most major enterprises—is not what Sanders is advocating for. And right now, America has a lot of socialism for the top tax brackets and hard, cold capitalism for wage earners, but that doesn't change the politics of the buzzword that Sanders loves and a lot of America hates.

This leads us to one of the major foreign policy issues that Sanders will have to address head-on during the 2020 Democratic primary debates, which is his past support for left-wing authoritarian dictators in Latin and Central America, whose regimes are actively in chaos or crackdown today. Sanders's visits as the mayor of Burlington and 1980s stances don't represent where he stands today, but issues in countries like Venezuela or Nicaragua are current, so he will be pressed hard by his opponents. He's also taking a new position on Israel as a Jewish American (though, he's not a religious person—another hurdle in itself) to be more critical of the Netanyahu-led country.

Senator Sanders is staking his foreign policy on opposing the spread of authoritarian right-wing dictators, and he has taken a public stance against Russian president Vladimir Putin, which is in line with party orthodoxy. Answering those questions will give him a chance to showcase his newly beefed-up foreign policy portfolio and a recent historic War Powers Act joint congressional resolution to check President Trump in Congress.

Another consistent theme of Sanders's politics over the years is that America spends too much money on the costs of war and not enough on the costs of building up our country. His congressional votes tell that story, and it's an argument he can fall back on.

Even though there are plenty of weaknesses in Sanders's candidacy, the positives seem to outweigh the negatives by far. Sanders really does care about all Americans, something his passionate fans and supporters love about him. His supporters seem to be committed for the long haul. You can't buy that sort of loyalty. It's earned through hard work and by earning people's respect and not backing down from a fight. It's the kind of fire and drive you need in your campaign to win elections and to lead America to a better, more progressive society.

The senator has some great ideas. His mind seems to ponder: How can we make most of America better? How can we make life easier for most Americans? What are some simple things that we can do to fix our country? What are some simple things that we can do to make sure that everybody has food on their table?

We shouldn't live in an "every person for themself" society. We are in this together. That's how Sanders seems to truly feel.

He wants us to imagine a society where teachers actually get paid. Where they don't have to work side jobs. Where they don't have to reach into their pockets and spend their own money on supplies for their students. Where the rich aren't the only ones benefiting from a great economy. Where there aren't any homeless veterans. And every American gets a fair shake. An America where we take care of each other.

It's good to have a politician who knows what his values are, something which is rare nowadays. It's rare to have a politician who's not running for office just to play politics or to pad his wallet. Someone who actually wants to make America better. Who wants us to be healthier and live more comfortable lives. Who truly wants Americans to not get screwed over by anyone. And someone who isn't afraid to fight for the little guy.

Overall, Sanders wants to make things better, not harder—not breadlines, not all this garbage that they're trying to throw out there about his "socialist" views. What he's trying to accomplish is to make things more fair for all Americans.

Sanders isn't trying to help members of Mar-a-Lago, and he's not just advocating for people who can afford $100,000 fund-raising gala tickets to get a photo. He's got a fully developed domestic agenda with legislation to back up his position and a comprehensive foreign policy plan to campaign on, a large base of passionate followers, and a social media presence large enough to rival the reach of a corporate media channel. He also has a groundswell of financial support, raising over $18 million via 900,000 contributions from 525,000 individual donors.[21]

So, Sanders has a lot going for him.

But there are two things he will need in order to have a shot at winning the nomination. First, he has to figure out a way to get former Hillary supporters to vote for him. Some people will never come around. That's just how it is. But we need someone who will be sure to unite us, rather than be used as a tool to divide us. And second, he needs to come up with a new word for his views instead of "socialism." He won't have enough time to redefine the word.

If he can accomplish those two things, then he has a clear shot to win not just the nomination, but the general election.

BERNIE SANDERS'S CANDIDACY

Senator Bernie Sanders led the Democratic 2020 presidential primary polls of declared candidates at the start of the campaign. He earned that early recognition by building a passionate following with voters during his career-defining run in the last Democratic presidential primary against Hillary Clinton.

As a 2016 presidential primary candidate, Bernie Sanders generated a tremendous wave of enthusiasm with his self-defined "democratic socialism" platform that stood on three main planks: creating a national "Medicare for All" health insurance system, providing student loan relief, and beginning a strong, government-backed reform of the big banks and the Wall Street financial establishment.

Sanders's campaign creates sharp contrasts with the other Democratic candidates, which isn't surprising since the senator has always remained independent, only joining the party to run for president. His supporters are legion, but it remains to be seen in next year's primary contests if "Bernie Mania" peaked during the last election cycle, still has room to grow, or if it's just enough to win a plurality in a packed field of candidates.[1]

Senator Sanders's political career is defined by his ideological firmness, which left him often as the sole dissenting vote in Congress and propelled him to a newfound popularity with the so-called millennial generation of voters. That effect was never more apparent than in 2016, when he ran against Hillary Clinton, whose brand of Democratic politics tended to be more centrist and corporate friendly after her twenty-five years in the public spotlight as first lady, then senator, and finally secretary of state.

During that primary, Sanders's brand took off even though the Democratic National Committee (DNC) held a limited schedule of debates late on weekend nights. But the Democratic Party divided along Sanders-versus-Clinton lines after the Russian government hacked and released the DNC's emails, thereby revealing that the party didn't believe anyone would mount a serious challenge to Clinton, certainly not an independent politician from a small Northeast state.

After his second place primary campaign, Sanders's progressive political ideas have swept through the Democratic Party like wildfire. And since then, Senator Sanders has toured the country with new DNC Chairman Tom Perez to advocate for party unity. He ran and won his 2018 reelection campaign as an independent after winning the Democratic primary[2] and refusing the party's nomination, as has been his custom.

Now, many of his Democratic primary opponents in 2020 and the party itself have adopted his central ideas of treating health care as a human right, his advocacy for a higher minimum wage, and making the U.S. income tax progressive again. Interestingly, most political scientists agree that Sanders's widely discussed ideology is not actually democratic socialism, but is better described as social democracy: a government with a strong social safety net but the means of production are generally privately owned, and the capitalist economy is policed forcefully with regulations aimed to create a level playing field and protect the most vulnerable Americans.

Bernie Sanders's campaign did not release detailed policy platforms at the early stages of the campaign, but he released his major policy positions in his twelve-point Agenda for America at the start of 2015. Many critics have pointed out that Sanders's plans are not detailed like those of his 2020 opponent Sen. Elizabeth Warren (D-MA), but American voters aren't always looking for detailed plans from presidential candidates when they know that the ultimate success or failure of an agenda lies in Congress. Both Sanders and Warren oppose the current way that America's free trade agreements are written, which sets them apart from the majority of both Democrats and Republicans.

The senator's primary agenda items of making the income tax code more progressive, breaking up America's "too big to fail" banks, and building a social safety net to eliminate poverty are mainstream liberal ideas. He also supports reviving the labor union movement in America, which has withered under a relentless Republican attack against collective bargaining. His foreign policy ideas have borne very real results recently, such as the Senate's resolution to end U.S. support for Saudi Arabia's war in Yemen. But some of his positions could hurt him with key Democratic constituencies in some states, like his long-term support for Venezuela's embattled President Maduro. So could his formerly NRA-friendly stance on gun laws.

Bernard Sanders started on the road to becoming a populist politician in New York City, where he was born to a Polish Jewish American family in 1941 just months before America's entry into World War II. His father was a salesman, who lost his brother—Bernie's uncle—in the Holocaust. That loss became an early defining event, teaching a young Bernie Sanders that "politics matter," as he'll frequently say. He grew up in Brooklyn and was educated in the city's well-regarded public school system.

Sanders's collegiate years would prove formative after he transferred to the University of Chicago and got involved in student civil rights activism. Intensely private, Sanders moved home to Brooklyn and then to Vermont, which is where he settled down after his son Levi was born. In the 1970s, his political activism led him to run for Senate as the candidate of the Vermont-only Liberty Union Party. He spent the next five years running for various offices until the party folded, but he built significant name recognition in the process.

By 1980, Sanders's relentless campaigning, using the same ideas he propounds today, led him to his first elective office. He won election to be the mayor of Burlington—Vermont's biggest city—by just ten votes. He drew national attention as "the red mayor in the Green Mountains" in *Rolling Stone* magazine, and his political profile grew as he continued to run for higher office. In 1990, voters sent the independent mayor to the U.S. House of Representatives as Vermont's sole member in his second run for the seat.

The following year, Representative Sanders founded the Congressional Progressive Caucus, which today is the largest House Caucus among Democratic legislators. Yet, he didn't join the House Democratic caucus. Still, Sanders enjoyed a good relationship with the Democratic Party as an outsider, gaining committee assignments and even chairing a House subcommittee.[3]

Representative Sanders served from 1991 to 2007 and claimed the title of the "roll-call vote" amendment king, borne out by actual research showing that he did win an unusual number of bill amendments to advance his policies, though he did not pass any major legislation. He also cast the lone vote against President Bush's war in Iraq, as well as engaging in a long-term fight against the post-9/11 surveillance expansion bill called the Patriot Act.

By the time Sen. Jim Jeffords (I-VT) announced that he wouldn't seek another term in 2005, Sanders was unopposed by Democratic candidates and trounced his Republican opponent. Vermont has elected him twice more to the Senate since then, by even larger margins.

As a senator, Sanders has passed one bill that he authored, and his relationship with the Democratic Party has grown closer. He sits on five different committees, formerly chaired the Committee on Veterans' Affairs, and is the ranking member on the powerful Committee on the Budget. However, it was the senator from Vermont's time as the Chairman of the Committee on Veterans' Affairs that led Sanders to his first authored legislation being passed and a major bipartisan VA reform bill, which he pragmatically ushered into law.

Senator Sanders has used his current high-profile assignment as the ranking member of the Committee on the Budget to criticize President Trump's budget proposals that are designed to benefit billionaires.[4] He contrasts himself with Trump by saying that the president is a "total phony and a total opportunist"and "he is doing what no president in modern history has done and really trying to divide the American people up based on the color of our skin or country we came from or religion or sexual orientation. That is outrageous."[5]

The Bernie 2016 political committee launched on April 30, 2015. Three and a half weeks later, Sanders officially declared his candidacy for president on Memorial Day in Burlington, Vermont. Little did anyone else know that he would go on to raise over $230,000,000 in the next sixteen months, and capture 46 percent of the national Democratic primary vote.[6] By September 2015, the Sanders campaign raked in over one million individual donations.

Sanders won New Hampshire's first primary and over thirteen million votes with majorities in twenty-one states. The Vermonter won a virtual sweep of the states in the Northwest, most of the states in the Midwest—besides Iowa's caucuses—and many of the states in the Northeast. Clinton's strength throughout the South and her victories in the large state primaries in Florida, New York, California, and Texas are what ultimately delivered her the nomination. Sanders still has work to do to win over Democratic primary voters in those states during this election cycle if he wants the nomination.

He would go on to endorse the Hillary for America campaign, appear at the Democratic National Convention, and even campaign for his former opponent leading up to the general election. Still, many party voters remain divided along the lines of that primary in the wake of Trump's shocking election victory, propelled by states that Sanders won, such as Michigan and Wisconsin.

After Trump's election, Sanders continued to maintain an active national profile by openly opposing the Trump administration and the GOP's congressional majority. That's when the Democratic Party largely moved in his ideological direction.

It was no surprise this time when Bernie Sanders declared his current campaign for president on February 19, 2019. Within twenty-four hours, his legion of supporters donated $5.9 million to the new campaign, in a reprise of the grassroots funding the senator used to out-raise Hillary Clinton four years earlier. When the Sanders campaign released its first-quarter fund-raising results for its first forty days, they revealed a tidal wave of funds from 525,000 donors across the country who contributed $18.2 million dollars.[7]

Bernie Sanders voters know what they'd get with the Vermont senator if elected: a tireless advocate for expanding the safety net and the pursuit of equality of opportunity in America who wants to reorient policy around people, not corporations or billionaires.

Notwithstanding his familiarity to most voters, Sanders will face increased scrutiny as a front-runner. He released his taxes in April 2019 for the first time in many years; they showed Sanders to be a millionaire himself. A media firestorm ensued. And he is going to face serious opposition research and media scrutiny for more than just his policy proposals in the 2020 presidential campaign, in which he's fighting against far more opponents. There are also lingering questions about his electability in inconclusive early polling which ask if Sanders can beat Trump in a head-to-head matchup.

There is no question that Senator Sanders can maintain a campaign throughout the 2020 Democratic primary. There is also no question that today, his policy plans are ascendant in the Democratic Party. For example, all of his opponents have adopted some form of universal health care. The big question is if Bernie Sanders can sustain his early lead, then build upon it to the point where he wins a majority of the primary votes and captures the Democratic presidential nomination or a plurality of votes and approval at the party's national convention.

DEFINING MOMENTS: THE 2016 ELECTION

Bernie Sanders maintained a national political profile from the time he won improbable election as the socialist mayor of Burlington. But he didn't become a household name until his even less likely smash-hit 2016 presidential primary campaign.

Sanders won twenty-three state contests and over thirteen million votes, vindicating the idea that there is a robust audience in the Democratic Party that is receptive to progressive politics.

In fact, that's the entire reason that the independent senator from Vermont took a leap of faith and entered the 2016 Democratic primary. Progressive radio host Bill Press—a former California Democratic Party chair and CNN personality—explained firsthand the early genesis of Bernie Sanders's first campaign in a recent radio interview with the author:

> *So I was talking to Bernie about talk radio and then when we finished, I said, now Bernie, what is this rumor I've heard you're thinking about maybe running for President? You know, Bernie said, "Come on. . . . Let's talk." So, he*

lays it out that . . . for him, it began as really a "message campaign."

I mean, he wanted to be sure that progressive issues such as Medicare for all, $15 minimum wage, were in the center of the Democratic debate in 2016 and he wasn't sure, in fact, he was sure that Hillary would not raise these issues on her own necessarily. So somebody had to do it. He had talked to Elizabeth Warren about maybe doing it and he just said, you know, if nobody else does it, you know, I'm thinking I may do it because they've got to get these issues out there.

Never expecting that it would take off. Never expecting to win for sure. And so my response was, if you're really serious, first of all, two things, number one, I said, Bernie, I'm really worried about this because I don't want another Ralph Nader, right. Somebody is going to jump in and then run as an independent and steal votes from whoever the Democrat is. Bernie said, I guarantee you I will not do that or do anything to help a Republican win the White House.

So then I said, well, you know, if you're really serious, you know you don't have anybody around you who's ever run a presidential campaign. You ought to get a few people. My suggestion is get a few people together who have had some experience here and get their advice whether they think it's totally crazy or not. And of course I should have known better. Bernie right away says, great idea. Would you organize that for me? So what can I say? We did!

Press hosted Senator Sanders and many of the people who would become his inner circle throughout the primary. If he hadn't, perhaps history would be different. Who's to say if the Bernie 2016 campaign would've even launched without those two political dinners in Bill Press's living room?

It's tough to say if even the people meeting with Sanders, whose Washington, DC, political career began as an outsider, was always an outlier, and whose politics were unabashedly different. Bill Press explained how the affair happened in detail:

[My wife] Carol cooked a great beef stew, we had Bernie and Jane and then one of his staff members, Michael Briggs, and I put together a dozen friends of mine who had been involved running presidential campaigns or doing media spots for them.

And Bernie just laid out his thinking as it had to be. And then we went around there and Tad Devine was there, who had run Bernie's Senate campaign, one of the key strategists who would at Bernie's request, kind of outlined what he thought was a little timetable.

And then Bernie just went around the room and asked everybody whether it was totally crazy or not. And you know, at that time we all thought, no, it wasn't totally *crazy. We agreed that was good to get these issues out there. We thought collectively that Bernie might be able to raise $50 million. We thought it was enough for Bernie to do what he wanted to do at the time.[1]*

That happened in April 2014. At the time, Hillary Clinton had no prospective challengers for the Democratic nomination for president.

Not only would Bernie Sanders reach the $50 million fund-raising target that his campaign manager proposed, he would exceed that number by 450 percent by the end of the campaign. He pretty much matched Clinton's primary fund-raising haul with $228 million to her $239 million, though she collected significantly more in donations through outside groups, which the Vermont senator generally shunned.[2] More than half of his donations were under $200.[3]

It's fair to say that Sanders's first primary campaign began in Bill Press's living room that spring day in 2014, except that it didn't. The radio host held a second skull session at his Washington, DC, home later in 2014. That's where the Vermont senator directly asked the members of Congress, his advisers and the political professionals he worked with to support his campaign for president in 2016, and they did:

And then a couple of months later Bernie called me and they said, "You know, that was really—I learned a lot. That was good. Good discussion. Can we do it again? Can we have another one?" So we did.

This time the menu was chicken cacciatore and we sat around the living room and had dinner and Bernie's now, you know, he's talked to other people now that he's been around the country a little bit. He's really seriously thinking about doing this now. What do you guys think again this time? You know, we went through it again and then at the end of that, this time we were joined, by the way, two members of Congress came, Keith Ellison, who was just elected attorney general of Minnesota, and Barbara Lee, congresswoman from Oakland, California.

And so this time we went around the table, room, again and then it at the end Bernie said, "Okay, Jane and I are going to," this was in November, "going to take the holidays and really think about this, but if I decide to go, will you be with me?" It was late 2014, but all assessed and everybody there said absolutely. And as they say, the rest is history.

Indeed, Sanders made history early in the 2016 campaign and there was no going back from that moment, which has defined the senator from Vermont's career since then. It led directly to his entry as a candidate in the 2020 Democratic primary.

On April 29, 2015, the Sanders campaign launched without fanfare, when he told the Associated Press that he was in the race. They tweeted the announcement.[4] A CNN poll at the time showed Bernie Sanders drawing

3 percent of the respondents. He told a group of assembled reporters that he would run in an area called the "Senate swamp," a grassy area near the Capitol parking lot. A month later he did a formal launch with five thousand people in attendance at Lake Champlain in Vermont.

By the end of the first month, Sanders realized that his campaign was really catching on when something strange happened while he was driving to give a campaign speech:

> The reality of what was happening dawned on Sanders when he got stuck in traffic on a Sunday morning. The senator from Vermont had launched his long-shot bid five days before. He was headed to a May 31 rally at the American Indian Center in Minneapolis, his first big campaign event outside his New England home turf. But Sanders was still blocks away—and the car he was in was not moving. "Is there a wreck ahead?" Sanders anxiously asked his field director, Phil Fiermonte. "No," Fiermonte replied, "they're here to see you." More than three thousand of them, many standing outside because the hall was full.
>
> "It never occurred to me in a million years that line was for us," Sanders recalled in a telephone interview Sunday, as his campaign bus chugged between Marshalltown and Ames on the eve of the Iowa caucuses. "I said, 'Whoa.' That was the first inkling that I had that this campaign was catching on."[5]

From the get-go, Sanders's campaign established a national base of small donors, many of whom became die-hard supporters and campaign volunteers. In just his first twenty-four hours, the Vermont senator raised $1.5 million, more than every declared GOP candidate at the time in their first day after launching.[6] He jumped the first hurdle of negative press during that time, when *Mother Jones* dug up his off-color writing from forty-five years earlier with a poorly written rape-fantasy satire and headlines about him as an oddball candidate supporting hitchhiking.[7] Still, in its first two months, Sanders raised $15 million from 250,000 donors at an average of just $33.51 per donation.[8]

By mid-July 2015, Sanders speeches were drawing vast crowds, including an eleven-thousand-person showing in Phoenix, Arizona.[9] It was double the crowd that GOP candidate Donald Trump drew at around the same time. That August, Sanders sold out the nineteen-thousand-seat Moda Center NBA arena in Portland, Oregon.[10]

Despite Sanders's rising national profile and Clinton's universal name recognition, the Democratic Party scheduled all of its primary debates at odd times and appeared uninterested in a competitive primary. "They scheduled debates on weekend nights, usually when there was some big ball game going on, right. Or a Friday night when nobody would be watching. And I don't know why because I kept making that point on my show," said Press, who asked the question that many Democrats wondered during the 2016 primary. "Why are they trying to protect Hillary from a debate? I mean, she's a great debater. You know, I think she won most of the debates when she's run for president both times."

Sanders also gave an interesting speech at Liberty University—a private evangelical Christian university generally favored by the GOP—about poverty and income inequality, seeking to find "common ground" and a respectful dialogue across the aisle, an unusual gesture during a party primary.[11] By the end of the third quarter of 2015, Bernie Sanders's campaign for president sent shock waves through the Democratic Party when he announced fund-raising in the amount of $26 million, only two million shy of Hillary Clinton's total for the same time period.[12]

The first Democratic debate wasn't held until October 2015, with the primaries looming just a few months away. It yielded a moment that would define the rest of the primary race, and in a way that ironically would later define the general election. After CNN's Anderson Cooper basically interrogated Clinton over her emails—a political red herring that the media never let go of—Bernie Sanders's grace on the big stage shone through. He replied:

> Let me say something that may not be great politics. I think the secretary is right . . . the American people are sick and tired of hearing about your damn emails. . . . I go around the country, talk to a whole lot of people. Middle class in this country is collapsing. We have 27 million people living in poverty. We have massive wealth and income inequality. Our trade policies have cost us millions of decent jobs. The American people want to know whether we're going to have a democracy or an oligarchy as a result of Citizens United. Enough of the e-mails. Let's talk about the real issues facing America.[13]

have done a far better job than we ha[...]

needs of their working families, the e[...]

the sick, and the poor. Democratic so[...]

we must create an economy that wo[...]

the very wealthy.[16]

At that point in November 2015, Sanders stil[...]
points in the polls.[17] But his fund-raising from[...]
million haul by the end of 2015 and an additio[...]
2016 alone, which allowed him to hire 139 orga[...]
170,000 Iowans participated; Hillary Clinton f[...]
cent of the delegate count and Sanders second[...]
Maryland governor Martin O'Malley earned 0[...]
dropped out.

New Hampshire famously holds the first [...]
tial election cycle, and success there—or in Iov[...]
sidered key to having a viable campaign. Su[...]
structural advantage there, with one of Verm[...]
the west side of the state. But what happene[...]
familiarity; Sanders's messaging was having a r[...]
Sanders won New Hampshire by a twenty-two[...]
ever recorded by a nonincumbent in that p[...]
Massachusetts governor Michael Dukakis's prio[...]
Clinton and Sanders tied among the party f[...]
voted for the senator by a wide margin, handin[...]

That weekend, *Saturday Night Live* parodied the debate and brought out comedian and showrunner Larry David, who created *Seinfeld* and *Curb Your Enthusiasm*, to play Bernie Sanders. The comedians re-created the famous emails moment and exposed the candidate to a vast new audience.[14] (Amazingly, PBS's *Finding Your Roots* revealed that Sanders and David are third or fourth cousins in 2017.[15]) Two former Democratic senators, Lincoln Chafee and James Webb, both dropped out of the race soon thereafter.

The following month Sanders gave a speech at Georgetown University explaining how his democratic socialism is an extension of the Democratic Party's New Deal policies from President Franklin D. Roosevelt in the 1930s.

In his inaugural remarks in January 1937, in the midst of the Great Depression, President Franklin Delano Roosevelt looked out at the nation and this is what he saw. He saw tens of millions of its citizens denied the basic necessities of life. He saw millions of families trying to live on incomes so meager that the pall of family disaster hung over them day by day. He saw millions denied education, recreation, and the opportunity to better their lot and the lot of their children. He saw millions lacking the means to buy the products they needed and by their poverty and lack of disposable income denying employment to many other millions. He saw one-third of a nation ill-housed, ill-clad, ill-nourished.

And he acted. Against the ferocious opposition of the ruling class of his day, people he called economic

royalists, Roosevelt implemented
that put millions of people back to
of poverty and restored their fait
redefined the relationship of the i
the people of our country. He com
and despair. He reinvigorated demo
the country. [. . .]

But here is a very hard truth th
edge and address: Despite a huge
and productivity, despite major gr
global economy, tens of millions
continue to lack the basic necess.
lions more struggle every day to pi
dard of living for their families. Th
last forty years the great middle cl
been in decline and faith in our p
extremely low. [. . .]

So let me define for you, simply
what democratic socialism mean:
what Franklin Delano Roosevelt sa
guaranteed economic rights for i
builds on what Martin Luther King,
he stated that, "This country has
and rugged individualism for the
success of many other countries

It was a tremendous accomplishment.

However, the Democratic primary shifted to more favorable territory for Hillary Clinton after the early contests, and she won the Nevada Caucus by a five-point margin later that month. Then, the crucial South Carolina primary delivered Clinton the kind of landslide victory she was expecting with over 72 percent of the votes.[20] She even won a larger share of the African American votes in that contest than Barack Obama had won in 2008.

On Super Tuesday, Sanders won four states including an expected landslide in his home state, broad victories in Minnesota and Colorado, and a narrow win in Oklahoma. Clinton brought home wins in seven states and American Samoa, including Texas, five other southern states, and Massachusetts. Overall, she gained 165 delegates more than Sanders did on that single day.[21]

The next round of mid-March 2016 primaries also favored Clinton heavily. She repeated her Super Tuesday result, gathering seven more state victories along with the Northern Marianas Islands, including two-thirds of the Florida vote, Illinois, Missouri, and three more southern states.[22] Bernie Sanders won four states, including Maine, Nebraska, and Kansas, but it was his unexpected triumph in Michigan that made headlines.

Clinton had been widely expected to win the Rust Belt
state, having led Sanders by double digits in polls lead-
ing up to Tuesday's primary. But the Sanders campaign
deemed Michigan a "critical showdown," and aggres-
sively attacked Clinton for her policies on trade and her

shock of all shocks, those very same ideas are now supported not only by Democratic candidates for president but by Democratic candidates all across the board from school board on up."[35]

The end result has been nothing short of transformation for Sanders, going from the outsider struggling to explain his positions to a 2020 front-runner facing a crowded field of opponents which reporters call "an army of Mini-Me's."[36]

Bernie Sanders has a firmly established ideology of promoting a strong social safety net and progressive taxation, which he calls "democratic socialism." His supporters see Sanders's long-standing beliefs as the cornerstone of their trust in the candidate, in addition to his track record of governing and even legislating pragmatically.

Senator Sanders has released a series of initiatives since the last Democratic primary—mostly over the course of late 2018 and early 2019—that add substance to his policy platform to support his twelve-point plan from the last election into a more complete agenda. He has also used the last two years to craft a foreign policy agenda focused upon opposing right-wing authoritarianism, on which he will run during the 2020 campaign. Its focus is on ending U.S. involvement in overseas wars, which culminated in Spring 2019 with a pair of resolution votes under the War Powers Act telling President Trump to stop supporting Saudi Arabia's war in Yemen. The Vermont senator's positions on Israel and Latin American affairs are sure to be discussed at the early Democratic primary debates.

Sanders's reliance on the moniker of democratic socialism is a big risk politically, since that is also the Republican Party's favorite anti-Democrat talking point. Moreover, his policy platforms do not include state ownership of most key private enterprises, which is the featured point of primarily socialist forms of government. Social democrats favor a strong safety net coupled with a capitalist private market, which is the basis of Sanders's politics that reflects the mixed form of economy, a condition that already exists in America.[37] In a mixed economy like we have in America, there are elements of capitalism with free markets allocating resources, and the government can intervene to achieve social goals. Ideologically, Bernie Sanders likes to jest—truthfully—that he's just to the right of former President Eisenhower, who presided over a 90 percent top tax bracket in the 1950s.[38]

As a senator, Sanders released the twelve-point Agenda for America in 2015 and started advocating for it throughout the ensuing Democratic presidential primary.[39] It still still outlines the basic positions he's advancing in 2020, and includes all of Bernie Sanders's main domestic political positions:

1. Rebuilding Our Crumbling Infrastructure
2. Reversing Climate Change
3. Creating Worker Co-ops
4. Growing the Trade Union Movement
5. Raising the Minimum Wage
6. Pay Equity for Women Workers
7. Trade Policies that Benefit American Workers
8. Making College Affordable for All
9. Taking on Wall Street
10. Health Care as a Right for All

During the end of 2018 and beginning of 2019, Senator Sanders cosponsored legislation to augment his twelve-point plan, which would raise the minimum wage, raise revenue through the estate tax on America's richest 588 people, and drastically lower prescription drug prices. When it comes to radical changes to America's institutions like expanding the Supreme Court or eliminating the Senate filibuster, Sanders opposes them, which might surprise some of his supporters. Overall, Bernie Sanders's policy positions are remarkably consistent in most domestic issues, except for his occasional past support for the gun industry, which still gives him a D-minus lifetime legislative rating from the National Rifle Association.

Since the last election, Senator Sanders has focused on foreign policy issues, even winning a bipartisan vote to carry out his agenda in a Republican-dominated body. However, his positions on Western Hemisphere relations could upset significant Democratic voting blocs. Since the Venezuelan hyper-inflation and refugee crisis began, he has backed slowly away from its socialist regime, but it's still uncertain if Latino Democratic primary voters in major urban centers will forgive Sanders.

HEALTH CARE AS A RIGHT FOR ALL

Health care is Sanders's tenth point in the Agenda for America, but in many ways it's his most important and most influential issue. Senator Sanders has consistently advocated for universal health care and recognizing the right to medical attention for sick people. All of the Democratic primary candidates in 2020 propose some form of universal health care, but Sanders takes his advocacy a step further, differentiating himself by rejecting the House Democrats' 2019 effort to put forward a bill strengthening Obamacare. His rejection is based on his belief that the time for incremental change is over, and that we need his Medicare for All proposal.

"The incremental [reform] that I support is phasing in Medicare for All . . . we would lower the eligibility age for Medicare from 65 to 55 and cover all of the children," Senator Sanders told MSNBC's Chris Hayes on March 27, 2019, "and by the way, expand Medicare coverage for elderly people to include dental care, eyeglasses, and hearing aids. That's the incremental four-year program that I wrote and that I support."

"Ultimately we have got to do [what] every other major country does and that is guaranteed health care to all, do it through public funding, save huge amounts of money and administrative costs. That's Medicare for all," Sanders concluded.

"This Sanders answer whether he would support House Dem legislation to improve ACA is pretty interesting," Hayes noted in a tweet about Sanders's new position.[1] "He says 'no' and says he doesn't support any incremental reforms, which is quite a departure from his record. He's voted for all kinds of incremental reforms including ACA."

In fact, Sanders's single-payer system would ultimately phase out private insurance from the marketplace altogether, including the markets established by Obamacare, which it would replace.[2] Other countries with universal health care—like Canada—still maintain significant markets for supplemental private insurance coverage, which is not mentioned in Sanders's Medicare for All plan.[3]

"The current debate over Medicare for All really has nothing to do with health care. It has everything to do with greed and profiteering. It is about whether we continue a dysfunctional system," said Senator Sanders at a press conference in Washington, DC, on April 10, 2019, formally introducing his Medicare for All plan.[4] Fourteen Democratic senators cosponsored his bill, including four of his primary opponents.

Sanders's new plan would include long-term care for seniors, in addition to dental and vision coverage, with the aim of phasing out private providers of primary health insurance and folding in all of the various programs, such as the S-CHIP federal program to insure low-income children that Hillary Clinton crafted in the 1990s. He pointed out that GoFundMe has become a prescribed part of America's broken health-care system, raising $650 million a year, and that other countries with universal health care spend roughly half as much per capita, though he neglected to mention that those nations achieve better outcomes.[5] If enacted by Congress, Sanders's bill would phase in Medicare for All over a four-year period.

"The Medicare for All Act will provide comprehensive health care to every man, woman, and child in our country—without out-of-pocket expenses. No more insurance premiums, deductibles, or copayments," the senator's summary explains, highlighting the business benefits of offloading the administrative costs of hiring benefits administrators to deal with the red tape from employer-based private insurance plans.[6] "A Medicare-for-all system not only benefits individuals and families, it would benefit the business community. Small- and medium-sized businesses would be free to focus on their core business goals instead of wasting precious energy and resources navigating an incredibly complex system to provide health insurance to their employees."

In March 2019, Senator Sanders reintroduced a bill aimed at expanding Community Health Centers with House Majority Whip James E. Clyburn (D-SC), who is the third-ranking member of his caucus.[7] The Community Health Centers and Primary Care Workforce Expansion Act would help 5.4 million Americans gain access to health care across eleven thousand communities and provide $4.5 billion in funds for capital improvements in the system.[8]

"Congressman Clyburn and I have worked together for a number of years and the result of that is that as part of the Affordable Care Act we were able to substantially expand access to Community Health Centers across the U.S.A.," said Sanders at the bill rollout.[9] "Health centers—importantly—not only provide primary care, but they also provide dental care . . . they provide low cost prescription drugs and they provide mental health counseling."

REBUILDING OUR CRUMBLING INFRASTRUCTURE

Bernie Sanders advocates for an infrastructure bill to provide jobs and ensure that American roads and bridges remain safe, noting that taxpayers have spent over $3 trillion on President Bush's "war of choice" in Iraq.

In early 2017, along with Democratic leaders, the senator released a "Blueprint to Rebuild America's Infrastructure," which would dedicate $1 trillion over a ten-year period to capital improvements.[10]

"Look, this is kind of a 'no-brainer.' Whether you are in the state of Vermont or the state of California, you understand that our infrastructure is crumbling: our roads, our bridges, our water systems, our wastewater plants, our airports, our levies, and our dams," Sanders told a Capitol news conference.[11] "When we rebuild our infrastructure, we rebuild the middle class because we can create up to 15 million decent-paying jobs in all areas of life: in urban America, in rural America, for all of our people."

REVERSING CLIMATE CHANGE

Sanders also includes combating climate change in his agenda, which means weatherizing homes and encouraging sustainable-energy projects like wind and solar power. Senator Sanders and former Senator Barbara Boxer (D-CA) once submitted a pair of bills to tax carbon and use that money to fuel a boom in sustainable energy, but neither got heard in committee.[12]

One of his senate aides told *E&E News* that Sanders's staff was preparing a "Green New Deal" in December 2018 before Rep. Alexandria Ocasio-Cortez (D-NY) released her own proposal with the same name in early 2019.[13] His primary opponent Senator Kamala Harris (D-CA) has also said she will create her own plan under that name, and Sanders's campaign told the *Washington Post* that their "Green New Deal" plan is also forthcoming.[14]

GROWING THE TRADE UNION MOVEMENT AND CREATING WORKER CO-OPS

A lesser known part of Sanders's policies is creating worker cooperative companies and incentives for people to own part of the businesses where they work, noting that ownership improves productivity and lowers absenteeism.

In addition, Senator Sanders has taken action to promote the health of America's trade unions and introduced legislation in 2018 with a House cosponsor that would eliminate key parts of federal labor law that allow states to weaken unions by passing "right to work" laws.[15] The senator's proposal would make it illegal for corporations to use union-busting techniques once half of the employees choose to form a collective bargaining unit and would sharply curtail the use of companies declaring their labor force independent contractors.

RAISING THE MINIMUM WAGE

Bernie Sanders has long advocated for raising the minimum wage to a "living wage," which is the measure of how much a worker must earn to afford the basics of housing, food, transportation, and health care. The federal minimum wage has stagnated at $7.25 for nearly ten years, though some states and cities have raised theirs. Sanders cosponsored a Democratic Party bill to raise the minimum wage to $15 in the beginning of 2019, which would phase in the increase over a six-year period.[16]

"Just a few short years ago, we were told that raising the minimum wage to $15 an hour was 'radical.' But a grassroots movement of millions of workers throughout this country refused to take 'no' for an answer," says Senator Sanders, who has long supported the minimum wage increases. "It is not a radical idea to say a job should lift you out of poverty, not keep you in it. The current $7.25 an hour federal minimum wage is a starvation wage. It must be increased to a living wage of $15 an hour."

Sanders and Rep. Ro Khanna (D-CA) took those ideas a step further with the Stop WALMART Act (Stop Welfare for Any Large Monopoly Amassing Revenue from Taxpayers Act), a piece of legislation aimed at ending corporate excess, unless the workers of some of America's largest companies pay them a $15-per-hour minimum wage.[17] The bill would prevent large public companies from buying back stock or paying their CEOs a multiple of more than 150 times the earnings of their lowest-paid employee, unless they give the higher wage and each employee gets seven days of paid sick leave.

"If Walmart can afford $20 billion for stock buybacks to enrich the likes of the Waltons, it can afford to raise the pay of its workers to a living wage," Senator Sanders's office wrote about the bill.[18] "It would cost Walmart $3.8 billion a year to raise its minimum wage to $15 an hour and would benefit nearly one million workers. Meanwhile, 55 percent of Walmart's associates are food insecure."

"The Walton family of Walmart is the wealthiest family in America, worth $180 billion," he tweeted about the perverse incentive for the retail giant using the earned income tax credit and food assistance to make up for underpaying Walmart's million-person workforce.[19] "Middle class taxpayers should not have to subsidize Walmart's horrendously low wages to the tune of at least $6.2 billion every year."

PAY EQUITY FOR WOMEN WORKERS

Sanders's agenda includes a bullet point about equal pay for women, but he hasn't introduced any legislation that would impact that problem. Plus, his prior campaign was twice accused of unequal treatment of women, an issue that the candidate discussed openly before his announcement in February 2019.[20, 21]

"To the women on my 2016 campaign who were harassed or mistreated, thank you, from the bottom of my heart, for speaking out. I apologize," Sanders tweeted in response to multiple negative articles about the upper echelon of his 2016 campaign advisers, three of whom did not return for the 2020 primary.[21, 23] "We can't just talk about ending sexism and discrimination. It must be a reality in our daily lives. That was clearly not the case in 2016."

In the end, Sanders let go of three of his top advisers and his campaign manager from the 2016 campaign.[24, 25] "We have been criticized, correctly so, for running a campaign that was too white and too male-oriented, and that is going to change," Sanders told *The Young Turks* in a recent interview.[26]

TRADE POLICIES THAT BENEFIT AMERICAN WORKERS

When it comes to trade policy, the Agenda for America reiterates Bernie Sanders's long-standing opposition to the way our country has handled trade deals for a generation. "I just want everybody to know, you're looking at a guy who voted against every one of these trade agreements," Sanders told a Kenosha, Wisconsin, audience during a December 2016 televised town hall on MSNBC.[27] "What was also clear to me is that the guys who wrote these trade agreements wanted very much to have the opportunity to shut down in Kenosha or in Vermont and move to Mexico and move to China, where they could pay people very low wages. You didn't need a PhD in economics to figure that one out."

It's important to note that Sanders does oppose the Trump trade war and his use of tariffs, though not all trade penalties, when a country dumps products into the U.S market, such as Chinese steelmakers.

"Donald Trump's haphazard and reckless plan to impose tariffs on Canada and the European Union is an absolute disaster that will cause unnecessary economic pain to farmers, manufacturers, and consumers in Vermont and throughout the country," Sanders said in response to the start of Trump's impositions of steep tariffs against China and Canada, a country that the president declared a national security risk without any basis.[28] "It simply makes no sense to start a trade war with Canada, the European Union, and others who are engaged in fair trade, are not cheating and where workers are paid a living wage with good benefits."

MAKING COLLEGE AFFORDABLE FOR ALL

The Agenda for America states that Sanders's goal is "making college affordable for all," but the policy he's most famous for—which has gained new popularity in the wake of the 2017 Republican tax bill—is giving existing student loan borrowers debt relief. When the Republican congressional majority and President Trump forced through an unpopular $2.3 trillion tax cut for corporations and the wealthiest taxpayers, they falsely claimed that the cuts would pay for themselves even though independent analysis showed otherwise, and that has been borne out by the results.[29, 30]

On the other hand, reversing the tax cut and implementing the Sanders plan to make college free would be cheaper, estimated at only $800 billion over ten years according to an analysis by the nonprofit Committee for a Responsible Federal Budget.[31] In contrast, his 2020 primary opponent Senator Amy Klobuchar (D-MN) told a CNN Town Hall that she's not in favor of free tuition.[32]

One of Sanders's major campaign issues is student loan debt relief, which has grown into a mainstream idea and could potentially add a lot of consumer buying power to the economy. The Sanders Institute is a think tank of the senator's political allies that presented a report by the nonprofit, nonpartisan Levy Economics Institute of Bard College that assesses the impact of a onetime debt forgiveness of the $1.4 trillion in outstanding money owed.[33, 34]

However, the Sanders campaign aides say that he prefers to implement a lower rate program for existing borrowers instead of complete debt forgiveness.[35]

Bernie Sanders's focus on issues affecting young Americans has generated a significant boost in his polling support from younger voters and in the subset of younger primary voters. His poll numbers are highest among college-age voters, and he won more votes in the 18–29 age demographic than Donald Trump and Hillary Clinton combined in the 2016 primary.[36] Unfortunately, turnout among younger voters is also regularly the lowest of all demographics, registering only 31 percent of the 2018 midterm elections vote and 51 percent of the last general election vote.[37]

TAKING ON WALL STREET

One of Senator Sanders's signature issues is breaking up America's so-called "too big to fail" banks. Large banks like Wells Fargo, Citibank, Chase, Bank of America, and U.S. Bank have all grown so large they fell under the 2010 Dodd-Frank financial reform act. Nonetheless, the Republican administration just released all of those large institutions from enhanced monitoring for systemic risk just a decade after a financial crisis sent the national economy into a tailspin.[38]

In response to the GOP's move to deregulate, Senator Sanders and Rep. Brad Sherman (D-CA) announced legislation in late 2018 that would break up those too-big-to-fail banks.[39]

"No financial institution should be so large that its failure would cause catastrophic risk to millions of Americans or to our nation's economic well being," Sanders said about the Too Big to Fail, Too Big to Exist Act.[40] "We must end, once and for all, the scheme that is nothing more than a free insurance policy for Wall Street: the policy of 'too big to fail.'"

Sanders's idea is supported by economists like MIT Professor Simon Johnson, who said, "The new Too Big to Fail, Too Big to Exist proposed legislation from Senator Bernie Sanders is short and to the point. The largest banks and other highly leveraged financial institutions are simply too big—and pose a real danger to our continued economic recovery."

PROTECTING THE MOST VULNERABLE AMERICANS

Another key initiative in Bernie Sanders's Agenda for America is strengthening Social Security. While the Republican Party continues to seek cuts to Social Security benefits, the senator has just sponsored a bill that would expand benefits for the poorest of seniors.[41] The Social Security Expansion Act is cosponsored by Sanders's 2020 Democratic primary opponents Senator Cory Booker (D-NJ), Senator Kirsten Gillibrand (D-NY), and Senator Harris.[42]

Sanders's bill would lift the cap on Social Security taxes, which only applies to the first $132,900 in annual income right now, thereby extending the program's solvency by an additional fifty-two years. An October 2016 Public Policy Polling survey cited on the senator's website indicates that 51 percent of Republicans supported expanding Social Security and 72 percent of Americans overall.

REAL TAX REFORM

The final item in Sanders's Agenda for America is "real tax reform" which the senator has followed up on by introducing an expansion of the estate tax. His For the 99.8 Percent Act would raise taxes on the top 0.2 percent of Americans in order to raise $2.2 trillion in projected revenues from the nation's 588 billionaires and approximately 1,700 wealthy families.[43] Republicans have sought to eliminate the estate tax, which Sanders estimates on his website will save the aforementioned Walton family approximately $63 billion in taxes, but he wants to raise the wealthy heirs' tax bill by $130 billion among others who would pay the tax.

"Our bill does what the American people want by substantially increasing the estate tax on the wealthiest families in this country and dramatically reducing wealth inequality. From a moral, economic, and political perspective, our nation will not thrive when so few have so much and so many have so little." Sanders said, explaining that his tax proposal would help close the income inequality gap.[44]

OTHER DOMESTIC POLICIES

Bernie Sanders has taken a contrarian approach to some of the more radical ideas being bandied about by the Democratic primary field when it comes to changing American institutions.

For starters, Sanders opposes the progressive idea of getting rid of the Senate's filibuster, the requirement that each piece of legislation needs sixty votes to advance. Republicans have already used "the nuclear option" to make every single presidential appointment a majority-only vote, which many commentators say has broken the institution.

But Senator Sanders isn't afraid to swim against the tide of his caucus to vote his conscience, nor take a stand on an issue.

CBS News's John Dickerson asked Senator Sanders if he was in favor of ditching the filibuster during a long-form interview as part of his presidential campaign launch, and he replied:[45]

> *No, I'm not crazy about getting rid of the filibuster. But I—I think the problem is people often talk about the lack of—comity—and the anger. The real issue is that you have in Washington a system which is dominated—by wealthy campaign contributors.*

That's not the only structural reform that Sanders opposes.

In an April 2019 public forum, the senator was asked if he was in favor of expanding the Supreme Court—which Congress holds the power to do—in order to right the wrong of Senate Majority leader Mitch McConnell's (R-KY) refusal to hold a vote on President Obama's final pick for the high court.

Again, Bernie Sanders demonstrated his willingness to buck the trendy answer and show that twenty-nine years in Washington hasn't changed his ideology or independence, but he has gained a certain institutionalism not associated with his former outsider persona. According to Reuters, he said,[46] "My worry is that the next time the Republicans are in power they will do the same thing, I think that is not the ultimate solution," in response to a question at a forum on Monday organized by public employee unions and other liberal groups. Sanders said he would consider proposals that created term limits for Supreme Court justices or would rotate judges between the highest court and the lower-level appeals courts.

On the matter of Puerto Rican statehood, Senator Sanders agrees with opponents Senator Elizabeth Warren (D-MA) and Sen. Harris that voters on the island should decide.[47]

Lastly, on the matter of the U.S. government paying slavery reparations, which has been an early question posed to all of the Democratic primary field, Sanders broke from the majority and declined to support the idea, saying "there are better ways to handle the matter than writing a check."[48] A month later, Sanders amended that stance to supporting a study.[49]

Bernie Sanders struggled in the last primary against Hillary Clinton—losing African American voters by a wide margin in the South, primarily due to her lengthier track record and name recognition—which is a reason why his new campaign has taken steps to emphasize diversity in 2020, while seeking to shed the past narrative of his difficulties with nonwhite voters.[50]

FOREIGN POLICY

Bernie Sanders's foreign policy positions were something of an afterthought during his 2016 Democratic primary campaign, which he began with zero aides dedicated to international issues.[51] Since then, Senator Sanders has made a pair of major foreign policy speeches, convened councils of advisers on the topics, and honed his messaging beyond the stage of generic rhetoric.

What sets the senator's foreign policy agenda apart from his numerous 2020 competitors is that he is coming off a major win at the outset of the campaign. In March 2019, Senator Sanders introduced a bipartisan resolution under the War Powers Act with Senator Mike Lee (R-UT), which directs the president to cease American involvement in Saudi Arabia's war in Yemen.[52]

He also relies on citing former President Dwight D. Eisenhower's warnings about the rise of the military-industrial complex in advocating for the reduction in global weapons spending, which is one of his domestic policy goals aimed at redirecting funds toward social programs. While Bernie Sanders used to be a supporter of Russia, even praising the Soviet state during the Cold War, his current stance has evolved to match mainstream thinking in the Democratic Party as news of President Vladimir Putin's 2016 election attack went from speculative to confirmed. He built that newfound opposition into a broader platform of opposing the spread of right-wing authoritarianism beginning with Trump and spreading to U.S. allies like Germany, Australia, and France.

Nonetheless, Sanders will face tough questions from his opponents and voters in states with heavy Latino populations about his stances toward left-wing authoritarian leaders like Nicaragua's Daniel Ortega and Venezuela's President Nicolás Maduro (and his predecessor Hugo Chávez), as well as about his comments on Cuba's communist regime under Fidel Castro. While his positions have evolved on South American and Central American affairs as times have changed and recent events in Venezuela have unfolded, his pro-socialism stances from the 1990s through this decade will provide fodder to his primary opponents.

At the outset of the 2020 primary, Sanders has also staked out new ground on the Israel-America relationship that tacks closer to the progressive movement's priorities and away from centrist thought in the Democratic Party.

Bernie Sanders clearly heard the criticisms of his 2016 campaign, during which he ducked foreign policy questions and pivoted back to domestic issues, and worked hard to create an ambitious and detailed foreign policy agenda. It was also a political necessity for Sanders to craft a detailed foreign policy agenda to compete with the early leader in 2020 Democratic primary polling, former vice president Joe Biden, who served on the Senate Foreign Relations Committee for decades and as its chairman for four years.

War Powers Act

In early April 2019, Senator Sanders achieved a historic victory in Congress, sponsoring a War Powers Act resolution to order the president to remove troops from Yemen. It's the first time that both houses of Congress have passed a resolution under the 1973 law intended to check the president's powers to deploy the military. Senate Joint Resolution 7 passed both houses with bipartisan majorities[53] after spending a year in transit, being passed in the Senate in late 2018 only to die in the House and get resurrected after Democrats took over the lower chamber.

Because Sanders is part of the Senate minority, his resolution required Republican support to pass, and GOP senators from Maine, Montana, Indiana, and Kentucky all voted for it, with the latter switching his vote from 2018 to 2019.[54] The House of Representatives passed Sanders's resolution with sixteen Republican votes in a 247–175 vote, which sends the matter to President Trump, who is expected to veto the legislation. Overall, it's a major accomplishment for Sanders to convince Congress to check the president's war-making powers for the first time.

"The time is long overdue for Congress to reassert its constitutional responsibility over war making. We need a serious national debate over when and where we put our military in harm's way, and about how much we are prepared to spend on those interventions," Sanders wrote in a *USA Today* op-ed with his cosponsor Sen. Lee just after the House passed their joint resolution. "Congress's historic vote on Yemen this week is an important beginning in that process, now we must continue forward."[55]

Foreign Policy Vision

His more detailed foreign policy approach began in September 2017, when Sanders visited Missouri's Westminster College to give a major speech in the same setting that Winston Churchill used to deliver his famous 1946 "Iron Curtain" speech. In a preview of what primary voters can expect to hear during the campaign, Sanders focused on opposing the global spread of that authoritarianism and white nationalism promoted by President Trump and his right-wing allies. He said:[56]

> We also see a rise in authoritarianism and right wing extremism—both domestic and foreign—which further weakens this order by exploiting and amplifying resentments, stoking intolerance and fanning ethnic and racial hatreds among those in our societies who are struggling. We saw this anti-democratic effort take place in the 2016

election right here in the United States, where we now know that the Russian government was engaged in a massive effort to undermine one of our greatest strengths: the integrity of our elections, and our faith in our own democracy.

I found it incredible, by the way, that when the President of the United States spoke before the United Nations on Monday, he did not even mention that outrage.

Well, I will. Today I say to Mr. Putin: we will not allow you to undermine American democracy or democracies around the world. In fact, our goal is to not only strengthen American democracy, but to work in solidarity with supporters of democracy around the globe, including in Russia. In the struggle of democracy versus authoritarianism, we intend to win.

That's a major about-face from Sanders about Russia, a country which he visited during the 1980s to create a sister cities program between his hometown of Burlington, Vermont, and the city of Yaroslavl, a program that exists to this day. It's also a break from the orthodoxy of his progressive base.[57]

At Westminster, Senator Sanders proceeded to lay out his vision for a noninterventionist policy, but one that isn't an isolationist agenda. He began by praising the United Nations and its work on attacking the root causes of international conflict, before explaining his multilateralist agenda:[58]

The goal is not for the United States to dominate the world. Nor, on the other hand, is our goal to withdraw from the international community and shirk our responsibilities under the banner of "America First." Our goal should be global engagement based on partnership, rather than dominance. This is better for our security, better for global stability, and better for facilitating the international cooperation necessary to meet shared challenges.

Far too often, American intervention and the use of American military power has produced unintended consequences which have caused incalculable harm. Yes, it is reasonably easy to engineer the overthrow of a government. It is far harder, however, to know the long term impact that that action will have.

Shortly after Churchill was right here in Westminster College, the United States developed an extremely radical foreign policy initiative called the Marshall Plan. Think about it for a moment: historically, when countries won terrible wars, they exacted retribution on the vanquished. But in 1948, the United States government did something absolutely unprecedented. We helped rebuild their economies, spending the equivalent of $130 billion just to reconstruct Western Europe after World War II. We also provided them support to reconstruct democratic societies.

That program was an amazing success. Today Germany, the country of the Holocaust, the country of Hitler's dictatorship, is now a strong democracy and the economic engine of Europe. Despite centuries of hostility, there has not been a major European war since World War II. That is an extraordinary foreign policy success that we have every right to be very proud of.

In October 2018, Sanders gave a second major foreign policy address to the Johns Hopkins School of Advanced International Studies. He again focused on the nexus between authoritarianism, oligarchy, and income inequality. But this time he cited some specific examples of the unsavory behavior of the Trump administration's allies and the result of its current decisions in the international arena. He said:[59]

Saudi Arabia is a country clearly inspired by Trump. This is a despotic dictatorship that does not tolerate dissent, that treats women as third-class citizens, and has spent the last several decades exporting a very extreme form of Islam around the world. Saudi Arabia is currently devastating the country of Yemen in a catastrophic war in alliance with the United States.

I would like to take a moment to note the disappearance of Saudi journalist Jamal Khashoggi, a critic of the Saudi government who was last seen entering the Saudi consulate in Istanbul, Turkey, last Tuesday. Over the weekend, Turkish authorities told reporters that they now believe Khashoggi was murdered in the Saudi consulate, and his body disposed of elsewhere. We need to know what happened here. If this is true, if the Saudi regime murdered a journalist critic in their own consulate, there must be accountability, and there must be an unequivocal condemnation by the United States. But it seems clear that Saudi Crown Prince Mohammad bin Salman feels emboldened by the Trump administration's unquestioning support.

Further, it is hard to imagine that a country like Saudi Arabia would have chosen to start a fight this past summer with Canada over a relatively mild human rights criticism [of] Muhammad bin Salman—who is very close with Presidential son-in-law Jared Kushner—did not believe that the United States would stay silent. Three years ago, who would have imagined that the United States would refuse to take sides between Canada, our democratic neighbor and second largest trading partner, and Saudi Arabia on an issue of human rights—but that is exactly what happened.

Latin American Foreign Policy Liabilities

Bernie Sanders's new policy of opposing authoritarianism has a glaring omission and it's almost certain to become a topic in the first 2020 Democratic primary debates to be held in Miami, Florida on June 26 and

27, 2019. That's because for many years, Sanders has supported and praised multiple left-wing regimes in the Caribbean, Central America, and South America whose socialism includes repression and human rights abuses. Sanders defined his support for those regimes as opposition to former President Ronald Reagan, whose administration actively intervened in the region—just as some of the farthest left elements of America's progressive movement define their foreign policy as opposition to President Trump today, which is a position Sanders does not currently support.

While Sanders was mayor of Burlington, he visited Nicaragua to meet with communist revolutionary Daniel Ortega, now the leader of the country. But today, Ortega is a strongman, and that's why Bernie Sanders faces regular fire for complimenting Ortega in the 1980s. Back then, he called Ortega "an impressive guy" and remarked about the Sandinistas' "intelligence and sincerity," arguing that they were not "political hacks;" the comments were discovered and released during the last Democratic primary campaign by *Buzzfeed News*."[60] Since 2007, Ortega has revised the country's constitution to rule by decree, abolished its strict presidential term limits, and suppressed political opposition with death squads.[61] *Jacobin Magazine,* the leading publication of democratic socialism, calls Ortega's self-enrichment in the early 1990s and current regime a "betrayal."[62] The Sanders campaign hasn't stated any new positions on Nicaragua, and the old footage has been nationally redistributed by Fox News since the start of his 2020 campaign.

What's clear from Sanders's statements in favor of the socialist Sandinista regime in the 1980s is that he didn't claim to be a foreign policy expert and his main premise back then was opposition to the kind of frequent U.S.

interventions that happened from the nineteenth century through the mid-1990s in Panama.[63] It's true that American policy in Central and South America revolved around the support of authoritarian, often military regimes.

Bernie Sanders's current policy on Cuba includes dropping the long-standing U.S. embargo of the island, supporting President Obama's 2014 restoration of diplomatic ties, and calling for an end to detentions at the Guantanamo Naval Base.[64] He even introduced the Freedom to Travel to Cuba Act in 2015 with ten Republican cosponsors, but it didn't get heard.[65]

But it's the senator's thirty-year-old comments about Castro that dominate the media discussion of his positions toward the island nation just ninety miles south of Florida. In the 1980s, Sanders also gave a full-throated defense and public approval of Fidel Castro's communist regime, which he pointed out did create a robust universal public health system. He said:

> In 1959 [. . .] everybody was totally convinced that Castro was the worst guy in the world and all of the Cuban people were going to rise up in rebellion against Fidel Castro. They forgot that he educated their kids, gave their kids healthcare, totally transformed the society. So they expected this tremendous uprising in Cuba," Sanders continued, but "it never came. And if they are expecting a tremendous uprising in Nicaragua, they are very, very, very mistaken."

> *Sanders insisted that he did not mean to suggest "that Fidel Castro and Cuba are perfect; they certainly are not." But "just because Ronald Reagan dislikes these people," he argued, "doesn't mean that people in their own nations feel the same way.*[66]

Even though Sanders was correct that no internal resistance or revolution arrived to overthrow the Castro regime, politically speaking, his statement will offend Cuba hard-liners since it didn't mention the island's total repression of free speech and jails full of political prisoners. He also omitted to mention that Cuba's "transformation" resulted in total dependence on Soviet aid by the time of his remarks, and that standards of living had fallen while islanders fled to Miami at any chance they could get. The *Miami Herald* reported in 2016 that Sanders said, "In a Third World region where thousands of peasants in most Latin countries are oppressed and starving, Cuba is a model of what a society could be," on March 28, 1989.

Ironically, the now-deceased Cuban leader Fidel Castro admitted that "the Cuban model doesn't even work for us anymore" in a 2010 interview with *The Atlantic*.[67] Bernie Sanders was confronted with his prior statements during a Democratic primary debate on March 9, 2016, and he replied:

> *The United States was wrong to try to invade Cuba, that the United States was wrong trying to support people to overthrow the Nicaraguan government, that the United*

States was wrong trying to overthrow in 1954, the govern-
ment—democratically elected government of Guatemala.
Throughout the history of our relationship with Latin
America we've operated under the so-called Monroe
Doctrine, and that said the United States had the right do
anything that they wanted to do in Latin America. So I
actually went to Nicaragua and I very shortly opposed the
Reagan administration's efforts to overthrow that govern-
ment. And I strongly opposed earlier Henry Kissinger and
the—to overthrow the government of Salvador Allende in
Chile.

I think the United States should be working with gov-
ernments around the world, not get involved in regime
change. And all of these actions, by the way, in Latin
America, brought forth a lot of very strong anti-American
sentiments. That's what that was about.[68]

"When I talk about democratic socialist, I'm not looking at Venezuela. I'm not looking at Cuba. I'm looking at countries like Denmark and Sweden," Sanders said at an MSNBC town hall in Nevada in 2016, but he will have to work hard to get primary voters to agree in light of the public endorsement he got from Venezuela's current President Nicolás Maduro during the last campaign.[69] Maduro told reporters on "Anti-Imperialism Day" that, "Bernie Sanders, our revolutionary friend, ought to win in the United States . . . If the elections were free . . . Bernie Sanders would be president of the United States," criticizing the U.S. electoral college system as unrepresentative of popular sentiment.[70]

Sanders's support for former Venezuelan President Hugo Chávez's unabashed socialist regime led him to publish a 2011 editorial from the *Valley News* tagged "Must Read" on his Senate website which has not aged well. It concluded:

> *These days, the American dream is more apt to be realized in South America, in places such as Ecuador, Venezuela and Argentina, where incomes are actually more equal today than they are in the land of Horatio Alger. Who's the banana republic now?*[71]

When the Clinton campaign brought up the issue in September 2015, he disparaged Chavez as "a dead communist dictator."[72] Maduro endorsed him later anyhow, but isn't likely to repeat that performance in the current election.

"So my view is that, whether it is Saudi Arabia, which is a despotic regime, or whether it is Venezuela, I think we have got to do everything that we can to create a democratic climate. But I do not believe in U.S. military intervention in those countries," said Sanders at a February 25, 2019, televised town hall on CNN with Wolf Blitzer.[73]

When asked directly by Blitzer why he "stopped short of calling Maduro a dictator," which he would not do in an interview with Univision's Jorge Ramos during an interview earlier that month, Sanders replied, "Well, I think it's fair to say that the last election was undemocratic, but there are still democratic operations taking place in that country. The point is, what I am calling for right now is internationally supervised, free elections." His answer omitted that the Organization of American States refused to recognize Maduro's most recent election, which is why National Assembly leader Juan Guaido declared the office vacant recently, leading to his diplomatic recognition by the United States, much of the E.U., and most of the nations of the Western Hemisphere as the legitimate leader of Venezuela.[74-76] Florida Democratic elected officials took public umbrage when Sanders refused to publicly recognize Guaido in the same Ramos interview.[77]

"My record is to be concerned about democracy all over the world. So we've got to do everything we can," Sanders said in conclusion at the CNN town hall. "But at the end of the day, it's going to be the people of Venezuela who determine the future of their country, not the United States of America." That position stands in opposition to the Democratic Socialists of America, an organization that is among the senator's top political backers.[78]

However, questions about Sanders's support for Latin American left-wing leaders are certain to arise once again in the 2020 primary debates because of ongoing humanitarian and political crisis in Venezuela and a decision he made in March 2019. That's when Sanders hired journalist David Sirota as a senior adviser and speechwriter. Sirota wrote a 2013 article in *Salon* entitled "Hugo Chavez's Economic Miracle."[79, 80] Since then, Venezuela's oil-driven economy has completely collapsed with the world's worst hyperinflation crisis and an outpouring of refugees has depleted 10 percent of the country's population in the face of starvation.

Venezuelan relations is the rare issue where Sanders is caught between the left wing of the Democratic Party and mainstream thought in his party. However, he is not taking a position thus far on Venezuelan issues solely in opposition to President Trump—as he did publicly in the 1980s when he was the mayor opposing President Reagan—which shows that his framing of foreign policy ideas have undergone an evolution in the last thirty years.

On Israel

Bernie Sanders is the only Jewish candidate currently running in the 2020 Democratic primary, and his position on the relationship between the United States and Israel breaks with bipartisan consensus, starting with his statements during the last primary race and more recently with his forceful support of the members of the Congressional Progressive Caucus. Sanders even lived in Israel on a farm collective (known as a kibbutz) in 1963, so he has a real connection to the country.[81]

Senator Sanders is "100 percent pro-Israel in the long run" but criticized Israeli Prime Minister Benjamin Netanyahu—who did politicize the relationship by aligning himself with the Republican Party—for failing to respect the rights of the Palestinian people.[82] "Of course Israel has a right to defend itself, but long term there will never be peace in that region unless the United States [recognizes] the serious problems that exist among the Palestinian people," he concluded. With that, Sanders became the first major presidential primary candidate to criticize a sitting leader of Israel.[83]

Since then, he has met with both Israeli and Palestinian activists working against Israel's occupation of the West Bank and criticized Netanyahu further.[84] The senator also supports President Obama's nuclear deal with Iran, which the Israeli government vehemently opposes along with its new allies in Saudi Arabia.[85, 86]

In January 2019, Sanders issued a statement that he is against the Boycott-Divest-Sanctions (BDS) movement that Palestinian activists support, though he voted against a bill that would've kept states from making hiring preferences based on support for the matter because of free speech issues.[87]

A month later, Sanders defended Rep. Ilhan Omar (D-MN) during a political firestorm after she made dubious comments about long-standing U.S. policy toward Israel, saying to *The Hill,* "Anti-Semitism is a hateful and dangerous ideology which must be vigorously opposed in the United States and around the world. We must not, however, equate anti-Semitism with legitimate criticism of the right-wing, Netanyahu government in Israel. Rather, we must develop an even-handed Middle East policy which brings Israelis and Palestinians together for a lasting peace."[88]

CONCLUSION

Bernie Sanders honed his messaging on domestic policy during the 2016 primary cycle and many of his key tenets have been adopted by the Democratic Party because of grassroots support for those issues. In late 2018 and early 2019, he followed through on that agenda with multiple pieces of legislation, many of which have House cosponsors from the Congressional Progressive Caucus, which he founded in 1991. Ever since Sanders's first presidential campaign, questions have lingered about his ability to translate policy ideas into an actual agenda which has a chance of getting passed. His recent push to introduce concrete legislation around his agenda provides answers.

Senator Sanders has worked diligently to expand his presence in the foreign policy arena and achieved a real success in just a couple of years. However, his past statements are going to be difficult to reconcile regardless of the kind of political explanations the Vermont senator propounds, and that could impact his primary results in states with large Latino populations like California, Texas, and Arizona, and especially in Florida. In addition, his positions on the relationship between the United States and Israel will place him in direct contrast with most of his competition, who support the current bipartisan approach. Sanders's branding on using the word socialism to describe his domestic policies is in opposition with most of the Democratic primary field, and the party itself.

Bernie Sanders's top challenge will be selling his ambitious domestic agenda to primary voters, while rolling out a foreign policy platform to rival several different areas of disagreement with mainstream thinking in the Democratic Party. It's not just a matter of policy disputes, but an issue of the politics of electability that Sanders must overcome due to the Republican Party's preference to make the election a fight about the buzzword of socialism rather than a fight about actual policy choices.

Within the field, he will also face a showdown with Sen. Warren over their aligned but differing domestic agendas. Her progressive platform is actually more ambitious than his, and more detailed. But Sanders's new-found and uncompromising view on health care puts him to the left of the entire Democratic field, who all propose universal health plans.[89] In a crowded field of 2020 Democratic candidates, it is apparent that Bernie Sanders has worked hard to stake out his own positions on policy issues and create a real alternative choice from other early front-runners, such as Biden, Senators Harris and Warren, and former U.S. Rep Beto O'Rourke (D-TX).

BACKGROUND AND EDUCATION

The path to the Senate for Bernie Sanders began with a typical upbringing in the Midwood neighborhood of Brooklyn, New York, where he was born on September 8, 1941. He and former vice president Joe Biden—along with the current Democratic Speaker of the House Nancy Pelosi—are all members of the "silent generation" who were born before the end of World War II, unlike our current president, who is from the "baby boom" generation.[1]

His father, Elias Sanders, had emigrated to America twenty years before his son's birth from what is now Poland, and was a paint salesman. His mother was the New York–born daughter of Polish and Russian immigrants.

Bernie Sanders has one brother named Larry, seven years older, and who gave him an emotional introduction at the 2016 Democratic National Convention.[2] The Sanders family never owned its own home, but always managed to get enough food on the table. In his DNC speech, his brother lamented that their parents both died young, but were both huge fans of the Democratic Party's 1930s New Deal politics led by President Franklin Delano Roosevelt. "But money was always a major issue within our family. It caused a lot of tension between my mother and my dad," Bernie Sanders explained in detail to *Vox*, "I became very aware of the importance of economics and what it does to people's families."[3]

As a Jewish American, Sanders was deeply impacted by the Holocaust, which took away his paternal uncle and much of his extended family overseas. The impact molded his view of politics, according to *Slate*, which he shared in a rare moment discussing himself on the 2020 campaign trail:

> *The second part of my life that shaped my views was being Jewish—is being Jewish. Crying when I would read books about the Holocaust, these picture books of what happened at Auschwitz and the other concentration camps, and tears would stream down my eyes. And it never occurred to me, I could never understand: Why would people do such terrible and horrible things to people?[4]*

Young Bernie Sanders attended P.S. 197 (New York City elementary schools have numbers, not names) as a child, where he was an athlete, something that later became his early claim to fame while attending James Madison High School in Brooklyn. By his sophomore year, Bernie Sanders was named cocaptain of his track team. He told CNN's Chris Cuomo during the 2016 campaign:

> *I was a very good athlete. I was pretty good basketball player. My elementary school in Brooklyn won the borough championship—hardly worth mentioning, but we did. And, yes, I did take third place in the New York*

City indoor one-mile race. I was a very good long-distance runner—not a great runner, but I was captain of my cross-country team, won a lot of cross-country meets and certainly won a lot of races.[5]

Yearbook records and newspaper reports in the *New York Times* showed that he finished eighteenth in New York City (third in his borough) running the one mile race and eventually became sole captain of the team.[6]

Sanders attended Brooklyn College in 1959 before transferring to the University of Chicago, which is where he discovered civil rights activism and socialism.[7] Admittedly not the best student, Sanders joined multiple activist groups and watched Dr. Martin Luther King Jr.'s 1963 "I Have a Dream" speech from the Mall in Washington, DC *Chicago Magazine* chronicled his college years, saying:

"When I went to the University of Chicago, I began to understand the futility of liberalism," he told a reporter for the Los Angeles Times in 1991. On campus, he joined the Young People's Socialist League, he became active in the Congress of Racial Equality (CORE), he was an organizer for the Student Nonviolent Coordinating Committee, and he organized and led a sit-in protest in 1962 against university-owned, racially segregated campus housing. He has admitted to being a middling student at U. of C., reading Marx and Freud on his own while investing lightly in preparing for classes and taking tests.[8]

University of Chicago students sent test renters to the school's housing to determine if they were making race-based decisions using the same techniques that became common after the Fair Housing Act banned housing discrimination six years later. When the university failed, that's when the the young New Yorker showed political courage and leadership for the first time:

> UC CORE organized a fifteen day sit-in aimed at convincing George Beadle—then president of the university and a 1958 Nobel Laureate for genetics research—to integrate the off-campus homes owned by the university. The University had bought nearly 10 percent of the homes in Hyde Park to combat a blatant racially motivated housing practice long since banned for spreading hatred known as "blockbusting," where realtors would scare away white families by claiming that black families would move in. But they kept the many rental apartments segregated, infuriating students for the school's hypocritical handling of the situation.
>
> Thirty-three students protested for those fifteen days. It made national news. Then finally, a compromise was reached, and Beadle addressed three hundred students with Bernie Sanders on the podium to announced a Committee to study the issue. But soon afterwards, a furious Sanders penned a piercing editorial about the "double cross" in the student newspaper—as you can see below—for refusing to answer tough questions as promised. The university bought time until final exams arrived,

so Bernie's forceful editorial noted that tables would be setup to solicit community comments and raise a few nickels (back then, nickels were worth something; the $25 fine would be equivalent to $195 today) and continue to use public pressure to force the university's hand.

Sanders later protested segregated restaurant service at Howard Johnson's, a.k.a. HoJo, in 1962, according to the Chicago Maroon, in nearby Cicero, Illinois. The following year, Sanders and 158 other UC Core members were arrested for resisting arrest racial equality protests at "south side" Chicago schools. Of the 159 protesters who were arrested, 22 were convicted with suspended fines, 133 protesters had their cases dismissed, and Bernie Sanders was one of four student equality protesters nailed with a hefty fine of $195 in today's terms, especially hefty on a college student's budget.[9]

Protesting for civil rights in early 1960s Chicago wasn't physically safe, and years later, Dr. Martin Luther King Jr. would say that, "I have never seen, even in Mississippi and Alabama, mobs as hateful as I've seen here in Chicago."[10]

Bernie Sanders got his bachelor's degree in political science in 1964, then spent half a year at an Israeli kibbutz before returning to the United States and becoming a Head Start early childhood educator for a brief amount of time. Then, he purchased a rustic summer home on an eighty-five-acre plot of land in Vermont near Montpelier for $2,500 with his first wife, Deborah,[11] who was his college sweetheart. The marriage ended in 1966, and Sanders would move to Vermont permanently in 1968 after his girlfriend, Susan Campbell Mott, gave birth to his son, Levi, in 1968.

During that time period before his first political campaign in 1972 is when Bernie Sanders went about writing numerous articles for the alternative newspaper the *Vermont Freeman* as an unpaid freelancer. While some of his stories stand out for their punchy themes such as "The Revolution is Life or Death" about the drudergy of nine-to-five jobs in New York, many of them are cringeworthy, but ultimately not reflective of any of the candidate's current views.[12] He was also a carpenter and a youth counselor, and he made filmstrips for the American People's Historical Society.[13]

In 1972, Bernie Sanders began his political career by running in a special election for Vermont's Senate seat for the independent Liberty Union Party.

He lost, but a career was born.

Sanders would run for governor as the Liberty Union candidate later in 1972, and again for the Senate in 1974. Sanders earned just over five thousand votes in that race, but a Democratic local district attorney named Patrick Leahy won that race; he is currently the senior senator from Vermont.

In 1976, the Liberty Union Party (LUP) reached its peak under Sanders when he won eleven thousand votes in the Vermont governor's race, good for 6.1 percent of the total vote, but he resigned from the party as its chairman in 1977 due to its inactivity between elections.[14] Since then, the LUP has only won three local elected positions in Vermont.

Three years later, Bernie Sanders entered the race that would change his fate, running for the mayorship of Burlington, the largest city in Vermont with a population of just over 37,000 residents in 1980. He defeated a five-term Democratic incumbent by promising to raise taxes 60 percent less than his opponent and won the race by a margin of ten votes.[15] As the *New York Times* reported in early March 1981 after the election:

> "I'm not going to war with the city's financial and business community and I know that there is little I can do from city hall to accomplish my dreams for society," said Mr. Sanders, whose election runs counter to both this state's native conservatism and the nation's trend toward the political right.
>
> Mr. Sanders did not campaign as a Socialist and Mr. Paquette did not make an issue of it. Nonetheless, Mr. Sanders's political beliefs are widely known, and he said of his victory: "Burlington will be on center stage because the country has gone in one direction and we have gone in the other."[16]

Mayor Sanders ran Burlington according to his principles, giving his unionized workers a 9 percent pay raise, but only 7.5 percent for their supervisors. "We're getting the workers involved in the day-to-day management," Sanders said, explaining his managerial style to the *New Republic* in 1983 before his first successful reelection bid. "These guys have worked here for years. They said, 'You can cut here, you can cut there.' They know."[17]

At the same time, Sanders used his mayorship as a springboard to foreign travel and to invite superstars of the left like Noam Chomsky to speak at city hall. But mostly, he governed pragmatically, taking care of the more mundane tasks in the smallest largest city in any state of the union.

Just before the dramatic conclusion of his first mayoral election, Bernie Sanders had met Jane (O'Meara) Driscoll, who would start working at the City of Burlington's Youth Office, and ultimately the couple got married in 1988.[18] Sanders helped raise her three children from another marriage, Heather, Carina, and Dave, as his own.[19]

In 1988, Sanders ran for the U.S. House of Representatives for the first time, when incumbent Republican Rep. Jim Jeffords quit the seat to run for the Senate. He won 38 percent of the vote, finishing second to the Republican former Lt. Governor Peter P. Smith, with a Democratic candidate winning 19 percent of the vote.

His mayoral term expired in April 1989 and Sanders left office and planned another run, first lecturing at Harvard University in the fall.[20]

In 1990, Bernie Sanders won his first federal election of ten when he defeated Rep. Smith by an end result of 56 percent to 39 percent and went on to serve sixteen years in the House of Representatives. Democrats stopped sponsoring candidates to run against him in 1994, which happened to be the only close race he has had since then, against his Republican opponent.

Jane Sanders became a force in Washington, DC after her husband took office, having a hand in the foundation of the Congressional Progressive Caucus. She authored over fifty bills and helped Representative Sanders pass an amendment to increase funding for low-income families to buy heating oil when the program was going to get cut.

Jane Sanders even had a hand in helping her husband get a minimum-wage increase passed after five years of advocacy, which the *Washington Post* praised in 1996 when she was named provost of Goddard College:

> *In 1991, Rep. Sanders began talking up an increase in the minimum wage. That is socialist babble, was the word. The bill became law this year. Those who predicted that Bernard and Jane Sanders would be too radical, too unyielding and too far-out Vermonty either to find a fit in Congress or to be able to build coalitions have been proven wrong.*[21]

Bernie Sanders proceeded to follow in Jeffords's footsteps in 2006, graduating from Vermont's sole U.S. Rep to become its junior senator, alongside Sen. Leahy. In 2004, Jane Sanders took over a school named Burlington College as its president, which she aggressively expanded, but ultimately went out of business five years after she left office. Donald Trump's state campaign chairman in Vermont complained about Burlington College's demise, which led to an FBI investigation; ultimately, no charges were filed and a Sanders adviser said the investigation cleared her of any wrongdoing in November 2018.[22] Senator Sanders won his most recent reelection to a third term in 2018 by a wide margin.

FROM MAYOR TO REPRESENTATIVE

When Mayor Bernie Sanders ran for the House of Representatives in Vermont for the first time in 1988, it marked the beginning of what would become his national political career as an independent congressman and the start of a partnership with his wife Jane that lasts to this day. He lost that year, but won his first of eleven federal elections only two years later when he joined the House of Representatives.

Five years after joining the House, Representative Sanders got his first major policy initiative passed. It was a minimum-wage-hike initiative, which is also a major agenda item in his 2020 Democratic primary campaign. He also founded the Congressional Progressive Caucus, which is a still-rising political force in national politics. Over time, he built a solid reputation for getting amendments added to bills to advance his agenda and eventually advertised his nickname of the "amendment king" during his last run for the Democratic nomination.[1] However, some of the political decisions Sanders made thirty years ago related to gun laws are sure to become fodder in the 2020 Democratic primary debates. Sanders also first marked his turf as an anti-war crusader during his time in the House, casting a pair of lonely votes that would age well, against going to war in Iraq. In 2003, a bill by Rep.

Sanders got incorporated into a major financial reform and is the reason every American can get a free annual credit report to this day.

On May 28, 1988, then-mayor Sanders married his current wife and adviser Jane. It was Memorial Day. The following day the couple left for the Soviet Union on a diplomatic mission to set up Burlington's sister city program with Yaroslavl.[2] Less than six months later, Sanders finished second in his first congressional election.[3]

He left the mayor's office six months later.

In the following 1990 election, Sanders defeated the Republican incumbent handily without a Democratic challenger to win Vermont's only seat in the U.S. House of Representatives.[4] Two decades of name recognition and mostly glowing reviews as the mayor of Burlington were the major parts of his successful race. Sanders also took a position against federal gun control as part of his campaign against Rep. Pete Smith, who himself reneged on campaign promises to oppose gun controls.[5] It wasn't an easy race, President George H. W. Bush appeared personally to try and bolster Smith's campaign. Smith had the advantage of incumbency, too.

It didn't matter.

"The basic message is, in Vermont we believe there is something wrong when the wealthiest one percent of the population has seen a doubling of real income over the last ten years while the middle class and the working class have lost ground," Sanders told the *Washington Post* after winning the 1990 election. "The voters were saying they believe Congress is out of touch with the needs of ordinary Americans—working people, poor people, the elderly—that they feel Congress is dominated by big money and they want to send somebody down there to fight for them."[6]

Bernie Sanders became the first independent member elected to Congress since the 1950s. He was accompanied to Washington, DC, in 1991 by his wife, Jane, who helped with many of his top early accomplishments as his unpaid chief of staff. A year after his election, the *New York Times* chronicled his early struggles in a story entitled "Political Outsider coping with Life as an Insider,"[7] which detailed how he gained a pair of committee assignments, decided by the parties, without being in a party himself.

From the outset, Rep. Sanders kept focused on pushing for his legislative priorities, which he wrote about in his 1997 memoir *Outsider in the House* in a chapter titled "We Win Some Victories":

> I have worked to raise the minimum wage from almost my first day in Congress. In 1993, I introduced a bill which would have immediately raised the minimum wage to $5.50 an hour and indexed it to inflation. . . . When I introduced my minimum wage legislation, I was only able to secure fifty cosponsors, almost all progressive Democrats. No Republicans signed on. President Clinton was also opposed, as I discovered at a meeting with him in the Oval Office. He said that he was not unsympathetic to the idea, but that it couldn't be done while his health care proposal was being debated.
>
> Despite the importance of the issue and the desperate straits of a core constituency of the electorate, there was practically no discussion in 1993 by the Democratic Party about raising the minimum wage. Now, in 1996, with a

presidential election coming up and tired of being on the defensive over the Republican agenda, the Democrats finally recognized it as a good political issue: polls showed that over 80 percent of the people were sympathetic to raising the minimum wage. To give the Democrats due credit, once they decided to push the issue, they did a very effective job.

In one of the few instances since Gingrich ascended to the Speaker's chair, the Republicans couldn't hold their members in line . . . six northern Republicans broke away from Gingrich and backed the legislation. Soon after, another fourteen Republicans were prepared to bolt with more waiting in the wings. The debate itself was quite extraordinary. In effect, Republicans argued that miserable wages are good for America because they keep the country competitive . . .

On August 2, 1996, the House finally gets a chance to vote on raising the minimum wage, and the measure passed overwhelmingly.[8]

President Clinton signed the increase into law on August 20, 1996, and the minimum wage was raised from $4.25 to $5.15, although future increases were not tied to inflation as Sanders's bill would've done, nor have they been since then. Still, that bill helped ten million Americans—71 percent of which were adults—and gave a tremendous boost to households in the bottom 20 percent of total income distribution.[9]

The central finding of an Economic Policy Institute study of the 1996 increase concluded that "the 1996–97 increase in the minimum wage has proven to be an effective tool for raising the earnings of low-wage workers without lowering their employment opportunities."[10]

As a congressman, Sanders got involved in numerous other bills, including the Northeast Interstate Dairy Compact to help establish minimum prices for milk, reflecting his state's mostly rural nature.[11] And Rep. Sanders also helped pass a 1992 act that established the National Program of Cancer Registries to collate medical information in a way that wasn't being done before.[12]

STARTING THE CONGRESSIONAL PROGRESSIVE CAUCUS

In 1993, Rep. Sanders and his wife cofounded the Congressional Progressive Caucus (CPC), which included future Speaker Nancy Pelosi (D-CA) in addition to other prominent long-term members who now serve as powerful committee chairpeople.[13] For example, House Committee on Financial Services Chairwoman Maxine Waters (D-CA) and House Judiciary Committee Chairman Jerrold Nadler (D-NY) are both CPC members.

The caucus had grown to thirty-four members by the time Republicans engineered a national landslide election with their "Contract for America" in November 1994's midterm election. The following year is when Sanders's caucus responded with the "Progressive Promise," an eleven-point agenda, and pushed back on the GOP's efforts in characteristically strong fashion when he said: "The more the American people learn about Speaker (Newt) Gingrich's Contract With America, the more we all realize that it is a fraud."[14]

Sanders chaired the CPC throughout his first decade in office. While it started with only five members, by the late 1990s, it grew to over fifty congresspeople and represented the Democratic Party's main alternative to President Clinton's Democratic Leadership Council, which advanced a more conservative brand of politics. Representative Sanders's comments from twenty-two years ago sound remarkably like his present platform:

> *Rep. Bernie Sanders of Vermont, Progressive Caucus chair, says progressives must "force debate on issues that conservatives and moderates prefer not to deal with." One issue that should be at the top of any serious national debate, he says, is the unfair distribution of wealth and income. The caucus will also continue its fight for a national health care system. "Health care," he says, "is a right, not a privilege." And progressives must address the fragility of American democracy, in which less than half the people vote, compared with 70 percent to 80 percent in Canada and Europe. Strengthening American democracy would entail not only reforming the campaign finance system, but giving potential voters a reason to go to the polls. Sanders also wants to address the subject of corporate control of the media. "I consider that to be a major issue," he says, "and the reason why people don't have a clue about how government works."*[15]

The CPC frequently fought against corporate welfare, the practice of giving large tax breaks and/or subsidies to large companies, while pushing the Republican Party to cease attacking Social Security and other earned benefits programs. By the late 1990s, it had grown to a fifty-eight-member organization, and even conservative organizations approached the CPC to find common ground on wasteful spending, though then-House Budget Committee Chairman Rep. John Kasich (R-OH) only adopted a couple of their suggestions to rein in pork-barrel spending.[16]

"THE AMENDMENT KING"

Bernie Sanders passed more "roll-call amendments" between 1995 and 2007, eighteen of them in total, which led *Rolling Stone* to call him the "amendment king" in a profile piece.[17] In fact, an examination of his legislative record shows that he passed forty-nine amendments in total during that twelve-year period, which began with the GOP taking control of the House and keeping it.[18] A roll-call amendment is when the entire House is forced to vote on the amendment to a bill, which is rare compared to many legislative amendments that are passed with unanimous consent.

An examination of those roll-call amendments offers a sampling of Representative Sanders's priorities:

- Transferring $11.7 million from the Naval Petroleum Reserve into the Low-Income Weatherization Assistance Program. [H.Amdt.1185—104th Congress (1995–1996)]

- Increasing funding for the Court of Veterans Appeals by $1.4 million [H.Amdt.1203—104th Congress (1995–1996)]
- Increasing funding for the Weatherization Assistance Program by $13 million and reducing Strategic Petroleum Reserve funding accordingly. [H.Amdt.270—106th Congress (1999–2000)]
- Increasing funding for the Low-Income Home Energy Assistance (LIHEAP) program and the Weatherization Assistance program. [H.Amdt.721—108th Congress (2003–2004)]

Another pair of roll-call amendments in 2002 and 2003 prevented the Bush administration from taking $320 million in pension disbursements away from 130,000 retired IBM workers.[19]

It's difficult to introduce amendments to a bill, having to get it past the opaque House Rules Committee in order to get a vote, but Bernie Sanders persisted and got those votes. Not all of them were counted, because some were unanimous. One example of a unanimous amendment that became law is a measure he proposed increasing funding for weatherization assistance grants by $15 million with offsets from other energy-conservation activities.[20] Another is an amendment the representative got passed into that made available an additional $100 million for federally qualified community health centers in 2002.[21]

Not every amendment to every bill is earthshaking, but over time they are an effective way for a legislator to move their agenda through Congress in bipartisan fashion, even when they're not the leading member of a majority party.

Unfortunately, one vote above all of the others Sanders cast during his eight terms and sixteen-year tenure in the House has the potential to discussed negatively on the 2020 campaign trail, and that is his "no" vote on the Brady Bill in 1991 against mandating a five-day waiting period on handgun purchases and against mandatory background checks for most purchasers.[22] It was a vote in accordance with his constituents' wishes at the time, but against the grain of his progressive platform over the years and a cause for criticism at the time. He voted against the Brady bill again in 1993, but it passed and became law anyway.[23]

One of Sanders's other votes from the start of his terms in Congress has become foundational and is sure to be discussed in a positive way on the 2020 Democratic primary campaign trail. In one of his first House roll calls, Rep. Sanders voted against authorizing President George H. W. Bush to go to war in Iraq on January 12, 1991.[24] Ten years later, Bernie Sanders would provide the sole "no" vote in the House's roll call to authorize the use of military force in Afghanistan after the 9/11 terrorist attacks, a war which has proven intractable for president of both parties.[25] Later, he voted against authorizing President George W. Bush's "war of choice" in Iraq, which is a decision that still divides Democrats and a war that America still cannot seem to get out of fighting now that it has spread to Syria.[26] Sanders also voted against NAFTA, which he rails against to this day for failing to protect American workers and favoring corporate profits.[27]

In 2003, Rep. Sanders's submitted a bill that became a key part of the GOP-sponsored Fair and Accurate Credit Transactions Act of 2003 (FACTA), which amended the Fair Credit Reporting Act and passed in both houses of Congress to become law.[28, 29] His bill required consumer credit agencies to provide a free copy of credit reports yearly. In response, Transunion, Experian, and Equifax established the website annualcreditreport.com. By 2010, nearly sixteen million individuals used Sanders's law to access their credit reports for free.[30]

As a U.S. Representative, Bernie Sanders showed that an independent socialist politician from Vermont could get things done on a national level, obtain bipartisan consensus to change policy, and build an institution that would outlast his time in the House. When Senator Jim Jeffords (I-VT) announced his decision to retire, Sanders announced his senatorial campaign in August 2005.

After twenty-five years in Vermont politics, the state's Democratic Party reacted to his announcement unusually: they did everything they could to clear the field for Sanders.[31] The decision for Democrats to back Rep. Sanders was an easy one, since he caucused with the House Democratic conference and polling showed that he was the odds on favorite to win. But it led to Democrats who filed to run in the party's primary claiming that the whole process was rigged against "outsider candidates." He was endorsed by former Vermont governor Howard Dean (D), who was then chairman of the Democratic National Committee, alongside Democratic senate leaders Harry Reid (D-NV) and Chuck Schumer (D-NY). At the time, it was the most expensive political race in Vermont history, with his main GOP opponent spending over $7.3 million mostly from his own pocket, and Sanders spending $5.5 million.[32]

In November 2006, Bernie Sanders won in a landslide, earning 171,638 votes representing more than 65 percent of the total against five other candidates. His former party—Liberty Union—ran a candidate against him who only received 801 votes.

SENATE CAREER

On the opening day of Congress, January 4, 2007, Bernie Sanders was sworn into office to become the junior senator from Vermont, after nearly twenty-five years of trying to achieve the office. Senator Sanders began his political career as an outsider, but now he would be inside a congressional majority for the first time.

That's how Senator Sanders would later got his first shot at chairing a committee, which he used to pass a major reform bill for the Veterans Administration. While he has a reputation for advancing an uncompromising ideology and political platform, the junior senator worked closely with Republican Senator John McCain from Arizona. And he would make his time in the majority count by passing his largest national initiative while in Congress in 2010 as part of President Obama's Affordable Care Act, a measure he is still seeking to expand as a Democratic primary candidate today.

Senator Sanders continued to use amendments to bills as a major vehicle to impact legislation, passing forty-seven amendments over his first two terms. Apparently, there is more consensus in the upper chamber, since only six of his amendments would require roll-call votes. That is how Sanders helped pass legislation to audit America's central bank, the Federal Reserve Bank.

After his 2016 Democratic primary run, the Senate Democratic Caucus did something that had never happened before: they welcomed an independent onto their Senate leadership team.

Unlike his improbable entry into the House of Representatives, where he arrived without a caucus or reputation, Senator Bernie Sanders started with a solid working relationship with Democratic leadership. Sanders even attended fund-raising events with the Democratic Senatorial Campaign Committee in the run-up to his more than two-to-one victory over his Republican opponent.[1]

That meant Sanders got the committee assignment he wanted the most when changing houses of Congress. The Democratic majority, led by Nevada Senator Harry Reid, made those assignments during the start of what became his eight-year term leading the chamber, and that in turn led directly to some of Sanders's top accomplishments. The senator-elect explained to *Mother Jones* from the House Rayburn Office building in November 2006 that he had a three-part agenda for his new office:

> *The first thing I want to do is to force reality onto the floor of the Senate so that we can end this stupid discussion about how great the American economy is. The economy is not great. The economy is a disaster for the middle class.*
>
> *Second, I want to focus on an issue that is almost never talked about on the floor—that is the power of big money. What are the moral implications? What do these people do when they have tremendous amounts of*

> *money? They use that money to perpetuate their own wealth and their own power. Every day, Congress works on behalf of big-money interests.*
>
> *Third, I want to take a look at some of the good things that are being done around the rest of the world that are almost never discussed in the United States. How often is it discussed that the American people work the longest hours of any industrialized country in the world? The two-week paid vacation is almost a thing of the past; meanwhile in Europe you get four to six weeks vacation, and maternity leave with pay. We don't know about these things. I want to take a look around the world and see what workers are receiving, and compare that to the United States—from an educational point of view.*[2]

Senator Sanders planned to force those discussions through committee hearings, in which he was helped by majority leader Reid, who appointed him to four committee positions.

He served on "Kennedy's" Committee on Health, Education, Labor, and Pensions (HELP) which is how Sanders referred to it, speaking about liberal lion, the Massachusetts Senator Ted Kennedy (D) who chaired the panel. Sanders served on the HELP committee's environment subpanel with Sen. Barbara Boxer (D-CA), with whom he would go on to introduce numerous progressive initiatives.

The junior senator from Vermont also was assigned to the Committee on Energy and Natural Resources and the Committee on Veterans'

Affairs that he later chaired, as well as his initial assignment to the powerful Committee on the Budget, which he is still on twelve years later as its ranking member.

It was an auspicious beginning.

CHAIRMAN OF THE SENATE COMMITTEE ON VETERANS' AFFAIRS

Senator Sanders remained independent of the Democratic Party but not its caucus, and he eventually rose to hold his first chairman's assignment overseeing the benefits and handling of all matters related to war veterans, an interesting assignment for an anti-war politician. A central role of the committee's work is overseeing the sprawling U.S. Department of Veterans Affairs (VA) and its more than 375,000 employees, its hospital system, and the distribution of benefits to soldiers who've left the military.

A major scandal enveloped the VA when it was revealed in 2014 that hospital administrators and lower-level staff conspired to cover up excessive wait times for health care at facilities around the country, leading to its admired Secretary Eric Shinseki resigning.[3] It fell on Senator Sanders's shoulders to do something about it as the new chairman of the Senate panel overseeing the VA, and his efforts to make a bipartisan solution get through Congress led *Huffington Post* to hail him as a "wide-eyed pragmatist" early in the 2016 Democratic primary.[4] Other efforts to pass VA legislation had failed, and Sanders's efforts were on the rocks, too, until he began hashing things out with his House counterpart Rep. Jeff Miller (R-FL) just one week after the two chairs had held competing press conferences declaring the other side to blame for failure of the bill.[5] What happened next was one of that Congress' few bipartisan measures, and its largest:

> *At a press conference on Monday, Sanders and Miller said the final deal would cost about $17 billion, with $10 billion of that devoted to covering the costs of veterans seeking health care outside of the VA network and $5 billion given to shoring up the VA's own system. In addition, $1.5 billion will go toward leasing twenty-seven major facilities in eighteen states and Puerto Rico. Miller said that $12 billion would be treated as "mandatory emergency money," while the remaining $5 billion would come from money already existing within the VA.*
>
> *"It may well be that some point in the future we will need more money, and that's a debate we are going to have to have when we cross that bridge," said Sanders. The bill as outlined on Monday would grant the VA secretary "complete authority to immediately fire corrupt or incompetent senior executives, while providing employees with streamlined appeal rights," according to a GOP aide.*
>
> *Sanders added that officials would have a 21-day window in which to appeal that firing—a provision that he insisted be included during negotiations. The bill would also include language expanding the availability of in-state tuition under the post GI bill as well as language*

that gives spouses of veterans killed in action scholarship opportunities under that same bill.[6]

Sen. McCain had helped Sanders author the Senate version of what ultimately passed as the Veterans' Access to Care through Choice, Accountability, and Transparency Act.[7] "Negotiating with Bernie was not a usual experience, because he is very passionate and he and I are both very strong-willed people and we spend a lot of time banging our fists on the table and having the occasional four-letter word," McCain said, praising Sanders alternation between f-bombs and negotiations. "But at the end of the day, Bernie was result-oriented."

"He is very open and honest as he goes through the process," said Rep. Miller, who told *Huffington Post* that the Vermont senator is a "realist" after their bill passed. "You know where Bernie is coming from."

Unfortunately, one of the reforms Sanders implemented that protected VA workers from arbitrary termination in the wake of the scandal wound up misapplied by the Merit Systems Protection Board when senior executives petitioned to reclaim their jobs.[8] Critics of Sanders's handling of the crisis believed he was overly defensive about the agency's poor performance, and he too admitted a problem during the 2016 Democratic primary, according to the *Military Times*:

Earlier this month, at a New Hampshire town hall event, Sanders acknowledged that "we should have acted sooner" on reports of wait-time problems and expressed regret that he didn't have a quicker solution for "those long waiting lines and the lies that some administrators were telling us."[9]

The ability for senior VA officials to retain their positions after the scandal has hurt reform efforts. Ultimately, Senator Bill Nelson (R-FL) introduced a measure to fix Sanders's fixes to the VA in May 2017 and it passed with a bipartisan majority in the House, and unanimous consent in the upper chamber.[10] Sanders didn't cosponsor the measure. It became law just two months later.

HEALTH CARE LEGISLATION

Long before Bernie Sanders became a senator, he advocated forcefully for universal health care in America. But when the Affordable Care Act was crafted in late 2009 and throughout 2010, he pragmatically chose to contribute to it, rather than reject its public-private structure altogether. In so doing, he won a massive victory for enhancing public health benefits that helps over six million Americans today.

As a member of the House, Sanders managed to appropriate $100 million extra to community health centers (CHCs) at the turn of the century. When the ACA arrived, he seized the opportunity to direct over $12 billion toward CHCs and voted for the legislation that ultimately became known as Obamacare. Michigan State University's *Extension* describes them thusly:

Beginning with just two health centers along the East Coast, today they are the largest, most successful

primary care system in America, offering not only medi-
cal services, but also dental and vision services, behav-
ioral treatment and pharmacies. There are centers located
in 9,200 communities serving over 23 million Americans,
including seven million children and 26,000 veterans.[11]

Four Key Components of Health Centers

1. Located in areas of high need: Health centers are constructed in areas designated as medically underserved areas or populations by the federal government.
2. Comprehensive set of services: Based on community needs, health centers offer medical, dental, vision, behavioral health and enabling services.
3. Open to everyone: Regardless of insurance status or ability to pay, health centers offer sliding fee scale options to low-income patients.
4. Patient-majority governing board: At least 51 percent of every health center's governing board must be made up of patients.

Sanders held out for more than just money for CHCs and in response to his claim that he "helped write Obamacare," which isn't entirely accurate, his senate staff did provide a litany of provisions he did get passed into law as part of the ACA:

Sanders's staff provided PolitiFact with several additional
examples of provisions the senator helped insert into the

Affordable Care Act, sometimes with the cooperation of other lawmakers. According to his staff, these include $1.5 billion in mandatory spending for the National Health Service Corps, a negotiated rulemaking process to redefine the criteria for designating medically under-served areas, a waiver for states that want to experiment on health care policy, a provision to double penalties for health care fraud, a provision strengthening the False Claims Act, language to make volunteer ambulance personnel and firefighters who perform emergency medical services eligible for grants and loans, a provision to ease payments to alternative medicine practitioners, higher funding levels for the Public Health and Prevention Fund, and a formula increase in Medicaid funding that bene-fited his home state of Vermont.[12]

In the end, Senator Sanders's efforts were rewarded when Rep. Jim Clyburn (D-SC) agreed to appropriate $9.5 billion toward the CHCs and $1.5 billion toward a fund to assist health workers who chose to work in the clinics.[13] Nearly one in five Vermonters receives health care at a CHC, so it makes a lot of sense why Senator Sanders chose to make a deal.[14] Without his vote, Obamacare would've never come to life. Because he chose pragmatism over ideology, the ACA passed, and his beloved community health clinics have prospered since then.

FINANCIAL REFORM

As a representative, Bernie Sanders acquired a reputation for using the amendment process to tack his priorities on to other bills, and he continued to do so in the Senate. One of the highest-profile amendments he succeeded in passing into law came about as part of the Dodd-Frank Wall Street Reform and Consumer Protection Act, when he worked with a backbench Republican representative from Texas. It led to the country finding out what really happened after the Bush administration's radical deregulation of investment banks led to a financial panic and crash, which in turn led to the Great Recession of 2008 and the subprime crisis.[15] Senator Sanders proposed the following amendment:[16]

> *To require the nonpartisan Government Accountability Office to conduct an independent audit of the Board of Governors of the Federal Reserve System that does not interfere with monetary policy, to let the American people know the names of the recipients of over $2,000,000,000,000 in taxpayer assistance from the Federal Reserve System, and for other purposes.*

The amendment passed with a 96–0 vote of the Senate with four abstentions and became part of the final law.[17] "It was a historic vote for the American people in terms of bringing transparency to what is perhaps the most powerful federal agency, 'The Fed.' I recall that on March 3rd, 2009 as a member of the Budget Committee, I asked [Federal Reserve Bank]

Chairman [Ben] Bernanke if he would simply tell me and the American people . . . which large financial institutions had received trillions of dollars of zero or near zero-interest rate loans," Sanders explained at a press conference right after the bill passed on May 11, 2010. "I thought that was a reasonable question, the American people had the right to know. Bernanke said, 'No, senator, I'm not going to tell you.' Well, with the passage of this amendment, the American people are finally going to learn which large powerful financial interests received trillions of dollars of zero or near-zero interest rate loans."[18]

OTHER LEGISLATIVE AMENDMENTS

Senator Sanders offered numerous other amendments that passed into law during his first two terms of office, including amendments to keep bailed out banks from outsourcing their jobs cosponsored by Senator Chuck Grassley (R-IA) and a law to get to the bottom of Gulf War syndrome:

- To require recipients of Troubled Asset Relief Program (TARP) funding to bail out the banks in 2008 to meet strict H-1B worker hiring standard to ensure non-displacement of U.S. workers. [S.Amdt. 306—111th Congress (2009–2010)]

- To require a pilot program on military family readiness and servicemember reintegration. [S.Amdt. 2905—110th Congress (2007–2008)]

- To provide, with an offset, and additional $15,000,000 Research, Development, Test, and Evaluation, Army, for a program of research on Gulf War illnesses. [S.Amdt. 3082—110th Congress (2007–2008)]

- To require that not less than 30 percent of the hot water demand for certain new or substantially modified Federal buildings be met through the installation and use of solar hot water heaters. [S.Amdt. 1525—110th Congress (2007–2008)]

- To require a report by the Commission to Strengthen Confidence in Congress regarding political contributions before and after the enactment of certain laws. [S.Amdt. 57—110th Congress (2007–2008)]

- To set aside funds for the Regional Test Centers for Solar Technologies of the Department of Energy. [S.Amdt. 2963—115th Congress (2017–2018)]

The pragmatic senator from Vermont also passed an amendment to one of Congress' broad appropriations bills which dedicated $350,000,000 to ensuring that his dairy farmer constituents didn't go out of business in 2009 due to the economic dislocations of the Great Recession.[19]

After the 2016 election, Senate Democrats gave Sanders a spot as their Outreach Chairman.[20] It's an important role, where his task is representing the views of the various committee chairs to Democratic leadership.

LEGISLATIVE IDEOLOGY

An independent analysis of the bills that Senator Sanders sponsored and cosponsored from 2015 through 2019 by the independent political website

GovTrack.us[21] rates him as the second most liberal member of the Senate. In comparison, his opponents in the 2020 Democratic primary are Sen. Amy Klobuchar (D-MN), who is rated the thirty-fourth most liberal senator, then Sen. Cory Booker (D-NJ) is ranked seventeenth most liberal, Sen. Elizabeth Warren (D-MA) is ranked thirteenth most liberal, and Sen. Harris is ranked fourth most liberal, while Sen. Kirsten Gillibrand (D-NY) is ranked the most liberal member of the Senate.

GovTrack's proprietary leadership rankings based upon how many bills he sponsored or cosponsored ranked him as submitting thirty-one bills in in the 115th Congress from 2017 to 2019, which is the tenth fewest bills out of his colleagues with ten years of experience or more. Sanders did cosponsor over three hundred bills, which indicates that he's willing to work collaboratively with others to achieve his goals. Their scorecard also reveals that only one of those bills had a cosponsor in committee leadership who would oversee the bill and he only had one GOP cosponsor on any of his bills. None of those bills became law in the 115th Congress.

Senators Sanders's bills had significant sponsorship in the House—likely due to his continuing, active presence as the Senate member of the Congressional Progressive Caucus—with fourteen of his bills sponsored in the lower chamber. Only one of his bills in the 115th Congress got voted out of committee and received floor votes, which passed the Senate: a resolution under the War Powers Act checking the president's participation in the war in Yemen. In the following Congress, both Houses passed Sanders's historic resolution.

Senator Sanders missed fifteen out of the 599 votes in the 115th Congress, which is 2.5 percent of the total over the 115th Congress' two-year term. In contrast, his opponent Sen. Warren didn't miss any votes during that two-year period, Sen. Harris missed only two votes, and Sen. Klobuchar missed three votes. Sen. Booker missed 4.7 percent of the total votes, twenty-eight in all over the same two-year span.

Sanders's 2018 reelection campaign did not offer any drama. Sanders won two-thirds of the vote in a nine-person field.

PREPARING TO RUN FOR PRESIDENT

"Our campaign is not only about defeating Donald Trump, the most dangerous president in modern American history," Senator Sanders wrote in an email to his supporters in February 2019. "It is not only about winning the Democratic nomination and the general election. Our campaign is about transforming our country and creating a government based on the principles of economic, social, racial, and environmental justice."[22]

He told the people of his home state first about launching his second presidential campaign on February 19, 2019, in an exclusive interview with Vermont Public Radio.

> Sanders said he is running to oppose President Donald Trump, and to enact many of the progressive ideas—including universal health care coverage, a $15 minimum wage and reducing student debt—that he championed in 2016.
>
> "I think the current occupant of the White House is an embarrassment to our country," Sanders said. "I think he

is a pathological liar. . . . I also think he is a racist, a sexist, a homophobe, a xenophobe, somebody who is gaining cheap political points by trying to pick on minorities, often undocumented immigrants."

Sanders acknowledged he will encounter a "very different campaign," than in 2016, when he emerged as the sole serious challenger to former Secretary of State Hillary Clinton and won 23 primaries and caucuses.[23]

One major difference between his first and second Democratic primary runs is that while Sanders wasn't sure if he was going to run in 2016 and only had a set of bullet points on his website to pitch as his domestic plans, this time, he has concrete plans in the form of legislation that he has submitted in the last twelve months to support his policy and show Americans what his presidency would look like.

Senator Sanders has filed or cosponsored the following bills since October 2018:

- The Too Big to Fail, Too Big to Exist Act of 2018, which would break up America's largest banks and regulate insurance companies that pose a systemic risk due to their extreme size.
- The Stop WALMART Act of 2018 to restrict large public companies who underpay their workers from buying back stock and giving those workers at least a seven-day paid vacation annually.
- The Raise the Wage Act of 2019, which would raise the national minimum wage to $15 an hour in several stages.

- The For the 99.8 Percent Act, which would raise $2 trillion in revenue by taxing the estates of billionaires and America's 1700 wealthiest families.

- The Social Security Expansion Act of 2019, which would boost payouts to the poorest recipients and extend the program's solvency for fifty-two years by removing the earnings cap from Social Security taxes.

- The Community Health Center and Primary Care Workforce Expansion Act of 2019, which would ensure that CHCs are funded for the next five years with a 10 percent annual increase that should result in 5.4 million Americans getting health care who otherwise wouldn't.[24]

As the junior senator from Vermont, Bernie Sanders has had an outsized impact on national legislation over his first two terms of office. He has impacted disparate issues in fields ranging from financial regulation to health care for lower-income people and veterans' health, and Sanders has crossed the aisle to get legislation passed to improve the lives of his constituents and the country as a whole.

Now that he's become the early front-runner in the 2020 Democratic primary, it won't take long for his original ideas or new political plans to become a topic for debate, which is a discussion that Sanders has been looking forward to having for decades.[25]

ANALYSIS: SANDERS'S CHANCES FOR WINNING THE NOMINATION AND PRESIDENCY

Bernie Sanders launched his 2020 Democratic primary campaign amid high expectations, and he has topped the polls of declared candidates ever since then, though he trails former vice president Joe Biden.[1] In contrast to 2016, the senator is adjusting to his status as an early front-runner: he leads the fund-raising race with $18 million raised and $28 million on hand, and he's got around a hundred staffers, 40 percent of whom are people of color and more than half of whom are women.[2]

Sanders is staking his campaign on his passionate fan base giving him enough early support to crowd out other candidates. He may be uniquely positioned to take advantage of the Democratic primary's proportional representation system, which only gives delegates to candidates who win more than 15 percent of the vote.[3]

Senator Sanders has also taken the time to flesh out many of his major policy priorities with legislation and a complete foreign policy platform—unlike his first campaign—as well as a complete launch of his signature "Medicare for All" initiative. Recent polling from the nonprofit Kaiser Family Foundation finds that public support is very high for his initiatives like health care as a right and eliminating the kinds of costly copayments and out-of-pocket expenses private care requires now, but people are wary of negative consequences like long wait times or tampering with the current Medicare benefits.[4]

"Bernie Sanders is kind of a phenom in the progressive and liberal movement," says *Politico*'s Marc Caputo, who is covering the 2020 primary campaign as a national correspondent, in an interview about Sanders's early campaign prospects. "A lot of reporters and a lot of elite opinion makers do themselves a disservice if they believe that Bernie Sanders doesn't have a prayer, because he certainly looks to be a pretty strong candidate, not only because of the built-in support network he had carrying over from 2020, and his ability to raise money which is really important in a state as big as Florida, but also because he's showing that he's learning from the mistakes of his past."

"Today, I want to welcome you to a campaign which says, loudly and clearly, that the underlying principles of our government will not be greed, hatred, and lies," Sanders said at an early campaign rally in Brooklyn, NY near where he grew up.[5] "My experience as a kid, living in a family that struggled economically, powerfully influenced my life and my values. Unlike Donald Trump, who shutdown the government and left 800,000 federal employees without income to pay the bills, I know what it's like to be in a family that lives paycheck to paycheck."

During his last campaign, Bernie Sanders was loath to open up about himself or his background, but during this primary he is making more of an effort to sell himself to voters and to tell his story alongside his policies.[6]

In April 2019, he is leading all declared candidates in all of the major polls—including national and Iowa polling—tracked by *Real Clear Politics*, though he is running behind Biden.[7]

"His chances are probably going to be better if there's a crowded field," says Caputo, who noted that polling in primaries is more erratic than general elections. "Bernie Sanders excites a certain type of voter that is kind of the progressive equivalent—not ideologically obviously—to some of those Donald Trump voters. Sanders is really one of the ones who kind of picked the lock of these small dollar donors, and showed how the new system to finance a political campaign could be run."

Bernie Sanders won the last Democratic primary in New Hampshire and this time around he is splitting the lead with Biden in four top polls, followed by Senator Kamala Harris, Senator Elizabeth Warren, and former Rep. Beto O'Rourke, in that order. However, CNN reports that only one out of every twenty voters is decided at this early stage in the race in April 2019.[8]

He's running second in the major Iowa polls, and the same in a February 2019 Emerson University poll of another crucial early primary state, South Carolina.[9, 10] A poll by the Institute of Politics of voters aged eighteen to twenty-nine found support for Sanders in 31 percent of respondents, followed by Biden at 20 percent, and O'Rourke at 10 percent, with no other candidate passing the 5 percent mark.[11]

Sanders won Wisconsin in 2016, and early polling in March 2019 shows that he has a whopping fifteen-point lead with 39 percent support over his nearest opponent, Joe Biden, but that primary contest is relatively late in the 2020 primary season.[12] In the last election, success in the four largest states eluded the Sanders campaign, and it was a key factor in swinging the nomination to Hillary Clinton.

A poll conducted in Florida by Bendixen & Amandi showed that Senator Sanders is in second place with 11 percent support as of March 2019, but trailing Biden by fifteen points.

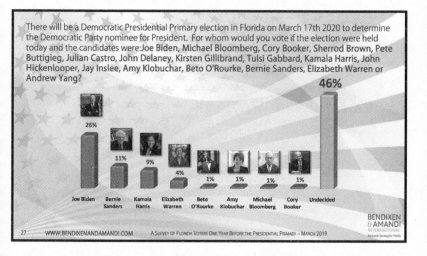

There will be a Democratic Presidential Primary election in Florida on March 17th 2020 to determine the Democratic Party nominee for President. For whom would you vote if the election were held today and the candidates were:Joe Biden, Michael Bloomberg, Cory Booker, Sherrod Brown, Pete Buttigieg, Julian Castro, John Delaney, Kirsten Gillibrand, Tulsi Gabbard, Kamala Harris, John Hickenlooper, Jay Inslee, Amy Klobuchar, Beto O'Rourke, Bernie Sanders, Elizabeth Warren or Andrew Yang?

Bernie Sanders lost all of the four largest states in 2016, and conventional wisdom is that he will have to improve his results in New York, Texas, California, and Florida in 2020 if he wants to win the Democratic nomination.

"The conventional wisdom is yes, Bernie Sanders would struggle in Florida in 2020, when you look at how he did in 2016. But it's important to remember that elections aren't static, that a future election is not a past election and a future candidate is not the same thing as a past candidate," says Caputo, who wrote an article for *Politico* titled, "'He is not going to be the nominee': Dems slam Sanders over Maduro stance."

"He is not going to be the nominee of the Democratic Party. He has demonstrated again that he does not understand this situation," Rep. Donna Shalala, a Miami Democrat who represents Venezuelan exiles, told Politico. *"I absolutely disagree with his imprecision in not saying Maduro must go." Shalala has filed legislation aimed at helping Venezuelan immigrants. The emerging issue hasn't yet spilled into the broader Democratic primary for president.*

Sen. Kirsten Gillibrand of New York and former Vice President Joe Biden, however, have clearly stated they consider Maduro a dictator and Guaidó the legitimate leader of Venezuela. And Sen. Elizabeth Warren told Pod Save America that she believed Maduro was a dictator and suggested she supported the "diplomatic part" of Trump's backing of Guaidó, though she faulted him for too much "saber rattling." One Democratic Hispanic consultant said the remarks will cause a needless "frenzy" in South Florida's Hispanic community.

Sanders did not embrace Maduro in his Tuesday interview with Univision's Jorge Ramos, who quickly touched on Guaidó being declared the interim president of Venezuela by the nation's National Assembly following Maduro's questionable election. But when he was asked whether he recognized Guaidó as the legitimate leader of the country, Sanders answered, "No." "There are serious questions about the recent election. There are many people who feel it was a fraudulent election," Sanders added. In a follow-up question, Ramos asked Sanders if he thought Maduro is a dictator who should step down. Sanders refused to say yes or no. "I think clearly he has been very, very abusive," Sanders replied. "That is a decision of the Venezuelan people, so I think, Jorge, there's got to be a free and fair election. But what must not happen is that the United States must not use military force and intervene again as it has done in the past in Latin America, as you recall, whether it was Chile or Brazil or the Dominican Republic or Guatemala."[13]

"I can assure you, that if he's the nominee, you won't be able to swing a dead cat in Florida without hearing about it out on the airwaves, or in some sort of publication. This was a major messaging issue, the socialism issue, to attack Andrew Gillum in the 2018 gubernatorial race. And considering how close it was, and considering how close Florida elections usually are, everything matters," says Caputo, who covered Florida politics for the *Miami Herald* for twelve years before moving to *Politico* in 2015. "However, congresswoman Shalala's criticism of Bernie Sanders: if you change her name to let's say, a Republican congressman, and you were to change his name to Trump, and you would change the date to 2016, it sounds like exactly something that was said in the Republican primaries, it's uncanny." He continued:

> Just like in the 2016 Republican primaries, Donald Trump was accused of not being a real Republican, of not being electable, neither as the nominee, nor as the general election candidate, and he was by and large loathed by the establishment. But lo and behold, he became the nominee. It's just these kind of uncanny photo negative echos that we're seeing again with the Sanders candidacy that I think is important to remember.
>
> Bernie Sanders as a candidate has shown an interest in rectifying some of the problems he had in 2016, which were some of the problems that haunted him in Florida, which are just minority outreach. He didn't do well with a lot of black and brown voters, that is with a lot of African American and Hispanic voters, who certainly, especially when it comes to African Americans, play a major role in Florida's democratic primaries which are close.
>
> And what we see now for Bernie Sanders moving into the 2020 cycle is his campaign is paying attention to that. He is doing black voter outreach. And it's a little early right now, I haven't really seen it, but I am certain

that considering the amount of black voter outreach he's
done, he's also going to do it for Hispanic voters as well.

"We have a strong field of candidates, and Bernie's entry makes the field even stronger," Senator Patrick Leahy (D-VT) said in a written statement to Vermont's *Seven Days* newspaper giving his endorsement on the first day of Sanders's campaign after withholding it in 2016.[14] "Bernie and I had a great talk today. I'm proud to support my fellow Vermonter, a proven leader with a strong message."

"There is profound economic insecurity. That is the sort of thing that happened in the late '20s and 1930s and that we overcame with New Deal democracy, which became a role model for market dynamism that was tempered by fairness for everybody," says Delaware Supreme Court justice Leo E. Strine, who is one of the most influential behind-the-scenes figures in American business.[15] "When we lampoon European social democracy, we're lampooning what we did to make the market economy work for all."

The 2020 Democratic primary race will go on for thirteen months before the first votes are cast in New Hampshire's primary some time before February 11, 2020. Primary campaigns are dynamic by their nature, and most often the early front-runner does not capture the party's nomination.

Bernie Sanders has improved his campaign platform and taken steps to rectify the issues his critics cited during the 2016 campaign. He starts with a tremendous advantage in name recognition, funding, and supporters compared to most of his eighteen opponents.

Early polling of a head-to-head matchup against Donald Trump shows Sanders winning, but the results are mostly inside the surveys' margin of error as of April 2019.[16]

Sanders has an objectively good chance of becoming the Democratic nominee in 2020, but he will have to distinguish himself from a large field, many of whom have adopted some or all of his platform. The senator's biggest hurdle is what happens if he wins a plurality of votes, but not a majority going into the Democratic National Convention, which would lead to a "brokered convention."[17] He's unlikely to be asked to be another candidate's running mate if he doesn't succeed, because he would be certain to overshadow the eventual candidate's profile.

Bernie Sanders can win the Democratic nomination. Candidates with strong ideologies who falter in their first primary have won the presidency by bringing their party around on their platform four years later; President Ronald Reagan's 1980 election is a solid historic example of this happening. Sanders's forceful rhetoric, his improbable rise from outsider to an insider who refuses to conform, and his empathy for the plight of America's middle class will make him a formidable candidate throughout the Democratic primary elections, and, maybe, in the general election.

NOTES

INTRODUCTION TO BERNIE SANDERS

1. "Congressional Progressive Caucus." Ballotpedia. Accessed April 8, 2019. https://ballotpedia.org/Congressional_Progressive_Caucus.
2. "2008 United States Presidential Election in Vermont." Wikipedia, the Free Encyclopedia. Last modified November 18, 2008. https://en.wikipedia.org /wiki/2008_United_States_presidential_election_in_Vermont.
3. Bade, Racheal. "Progressives Back Pelosi for Speaker—in Return for More Power." *Politico*. Last modified November 16, 2018. https://www.politico .com/story/2018/11/16/pelosi-speaker-progressives-congress-998595.
4. "Twitter Post." Welcome to Twitter. Accessed April 8, 2019. https://twitter .com/aoc/status/1065335143529877505.
5. "Classic Bernie Sanders–1988 Interview–Individuals with Money Dominate the Political Process." C-SPAN.org. Accessed April 8, 2019. https://www .c-span.org/video/?c4539766/classic-bernie-sanders-1988-interview-individuals -money-dominate-political-process.
6. Levitz, Eric. "The Radical Left's Agenda Is More Popular Than the Mainstream GOP's." *Intelligencer*. Last modified August 2, 2018. http:// nymag.com/intelligencer/amp/2018/08/the-radical-lefts-agend-is-more -popular-than-the-gops.html.
7. "Two-Year Extension of the Community Health Center Fund." Every CRS Report–EveryCRSReport.com. Last modified October 18, 2017. https:// www.everycrsreport.com/reports/IN10804.html.
8. "Bernie Sanders on Universal Healthcare, 1991." C-SPAN.org. Accessed April 8, 2019. https://www.c-span.org/video/?c4582581/bernie-sanders -universal-healthcare-1991.
9. "Twitter Post." Welcome to Twitter. Accessed April 8, 2019. https://twitter .com/cascamike/status/708714719675199488.

10. "Twitter Post." Welcome to Twitter. Accessed April 8, 2019. https://twitter .com/BernieSanders/status/687317650658189312.

11. Merica, Dan. "Sanders Aides Dispute Clinton Claim That Senator Was Absent in '90s Health Care Fights." CNN. Last modified March 13, 2016. https://www.cnn.com/2016/03/12/politics/hillary-clinton-bernie-sanders -health-care/index.html.

12. Helmer, Lizzie. "Bernie Sanders Hammers EPA Nominee to Give a Straight Answer on Climate Change." *IJR*. Last modified January 16, 2019. https:// ijr.com/bernie-sanders-epa-wheeler-climate-change/.

13. Turner, Cory. "School Vouchers, Oligarchy and Grizzlies: Highlights from the DeVos Hearing." NPR.org. Last modified January 18, 2017. https:// www.npr.org/sections/ed/2017/01/18/510417234/the-devos-hearing-in-their -own-words.

14. Margolis, Jon. "Bernie of Burlington." *New Republic*. Last modified March 14, 1983. https://newrepublic.com/article/122285/bernie-burlington.

15. Debenedetti, Gabriel. "Bernie Sanders Is Quietly Building a Digital Media Empire." *Intelligencer*. Last modified April 22, 2018. http://nymag.com /intelligencer/2018/04/bernie-sanders-is-quietly-building-a-digital-media -empire.html.

16. Golshan, Tara. "The Anti–Bernie Sanders Campaign Being Pushed by Former Clinton Staffers, Explained." *Vox*. Last modified March 8, 2019. https://www.vox.com/2019/3/8/18253459/hillary-clinton-bernie-sanders -2020-relitigate-primary.

17. Collins, Michael. "Indictment: Russians Also Tried to Help Bernie Sanders, Jill Stein Presidential Campaigns." *USA Today*. Last modified February 17, 2018. https://www.usatoday.com/story/news/politics/2018/02/17/indictment -russians-also-tried-help-bernie-sanders-jill-stein-presidential-campaigns /348051002/.

18. Seitz-Wald, Alex. "Bernie Sanders Staff Shake-up: Top Strategists Leave His Presidential Campaign." *NBC News*. Last modified February 26, 2019. https://www.nbcnews.com/politics/2020-election/bernie-sanders-staff -shakeup-top-strategists-leave-his-presidential-campaign-n976221.

19. Blake, Aaron. "Is socialism on the rise in the United States?" *Washington Post*. Last modified February 7, 2019. https://www.washingtonpost.com /politics/2019/02/07/is-socialism-rise-united-states/?noredirect=on&utm _term=.8e8c2cf95f9c.

20. Montanaro, Domenico, and Mara Liasson. "Trump's 'Socialism' Attack on Democrats Has Its Roots in Cold War Fear." NPR.org. Last modified February 12, 2019. https://www.npr.org/2019/02/12/693618375/socialism -vs-greatness-for-trump-that-s-2020-in-a-nutshell.

21. Otterbein, Holly. "Sanders Raises $18 Million in First Quarter of Presidential Campaign." *Politico*. Last modified April 2, 2019. https://www .politico.com/story/2019/04/02/bernie-sanders-2020-campaign-fund -raising-1248075.

BERNIE SANDERS'S CANDIDACY

1. Barnicle, Mike. "Bernie Mania Is Real and Powerful." *The Daily Beast*. Last modified January 24, 2016. https://www.thedailybeast.com/bernie-mania -is-real-and-powerful.

2. Isaac Dovere, Edward. "Sanders to Run As a Democrat but Not Accept Nomination." *Politico*. Last modified May 21, 2018. https://www.politico .com/story/2018/05/21/bernie-sanders-democrat-independent-vermont -601844.

3. "Congressional Progressive Caucus: What is CPC?" Congressional Progressive Caucus: Home. Accessed April 8, 2019. https://cpc-grijalva .house.gov/what-is-cpc/.

4. WCAX. "Sanders: Trump Budget Designed to Benefit Billionaires." Home. Accessed April 8, 2019. https://www.wcax.com/content/news/Sanders -Trump-budget-designed-to-benefit-billionaires-507744551.html.

5. "Twitter Post." Welcome to Twitter. Accessed April 8, 2019. https://twitter .com/NewDay/status/1067396567215165440.

6. "BERNIE 2016." FEC.gov. Accessed April 8, 2019. https://www.fec.gov /data/committee/C00577130/?cycle=2016.

7. Hohmann, James. "The Daily 202: Bernie Sanders is more pragmatic than you may think." *Washington Post*. Last modified April 2, 2019. https:// www.washingtonpost.com/news/powerpost/paloma/daily-202/2019/04 /02/daily-202-bernie-sanders-is-more-pragmatic-than-you-may-think /5ca2b7371b326b0f7f38f2e3/?utm_term=.c31362daa9fa.

DEFINING MOMENTS: THE 2016 ELECTION

1. Stern, Grant. "An interview with Bill Press about his book 'From the Left: A life in the Crossfire'" B. *Jacobs vs. Goliath radio show*. November 14, 2018.

2. Stewart, Josh. "Following the Money Behind the Nearly $500 Million 2016 Democratic Primary." Sunlight Foundation. Last modified October 26, 2016. https://sunlightfoundation.com/2016/06/21/following-the-money -behind-the-nearly-500-million-2016-democratic-primary/.

3. OpenSecrets.org. "Summary Data for Bernie Sanders, 2016 Cycle." *Open Secrets*. Accessed April 11, 2019. https://www.opensecrets.org/pres16 /candidate?id=N00000528.

4. The Associated Press. "Twitter Post." Welcome to Twitter. Accessed April 11, 2019. https://twitter.com/AP/status/593566088685875201.

5. Tumulty, Karen. "How Sanders caught fire in Iowa and turned the Clinton coronation into a real race." *Washington Post*. Last modified February 2, 2016. https://www.washingtonpost.com/politics/how-sanders-caught-fire -in-iowa-and-turned-the-clinton-coronation-into-a-real-race/2016/02/02 /83b08d22-c79a-11e5-8965-0607e0e265ce_story.html?utm_term =.7f6520a9634d.

6. Merica, Dan. "Bernie Sanders Raises $1.5 Million in 24 Hours Politics." CNN. Last modified May 1, 2015. http://www.cnn.com/2015/05/01 /politics/bernie-sanders-fund-raising/.

7. Murphy, Tim. "How Bernie Sanders Learned to Be a Real Politician." *Mother Jones*. Last modified February 19, 2019. https://www.motherjones .com/politics/2015/05/young-bernie-sanders -liberty-union-vermont/.

8. Merica, Dan. "Bernie Sanders's Campaign Raises $15 Million." CNN. Last modified July 2, 2015. https://www.cnn.com/2015/07/02/politics/bernie -sanders-fund-raising/index.html.

9. Wagner, John. "Bernie Sanders draws his biggest crowd yet—in Arizona of all places." *Washington Post*. Last modified July 19, 2015. https://www .washingtonpost.com/news/post-politics/wp/2015/07/19/bernie-sanders -draws-his-biggest-crowd-yet-in-arizona-of-all-places/.

10. Merica, Dan. "Bernie Sanders Draws Biggest Crowd with Portland Rally Politics." CNN. Last modified August 10, 2015. https://www.cnn.com /2015/08/10/politics/bernie-sanders-portland-rally-19000-2016/index.html.

11. Corasaniti, Nick. "Bernie Sanders Makes Rare Appeal to Evangelicals at Liberty University." *First Draft*. Accessed April 11, 2019. https://www

.nytimes.com/politics/first-draft/2015/09/14/bernie-sanders-makes-rare
-appeal-to-evangelicals-at-liberty-university/.

12. Gold, Matea, and John Wagner. "Sanders nearly matches Clinton in fund-raising for third quarter." *Washington Post*. Last modified September 30, 2015. https://www.washingtonpost.com/politics/heading-into-primaries -sanders-raises-24-million-in-3rd-quarter/2015/09/30/ef061a36-67ac-11e5 -8325-a42b5a459b1e_story.html?utm_term=.e96de2f524cc.

13. *Washington Post* Staff. "The CNN Democratic debate transcript, anno-tated." *Washington Post*. Last modified October 13, 2015. https://www .washingtonpost.com/news/the-fix/wp/2015/10/13/the-oct-13-democratic -debate-who-said-what-and-what-it-means/?utm_term=.198edea6be93.

14. "Democratic Debate Cold Open–SNL." YouTube. Last modified October 18, 2015. https://www.youtube.com/watch?v=pfmwGAd1L-o.

15. Pierce, Scott D. "Mormon Records Helped Uncover Family Histories for Bernie Sanders and Larry David." The Salt Lake Tribune. Last modified October 2, 2017. https://www.sltrib.com/news/2017/10/02/mormon-records -helped-uncover-family-histories-for-bernie-sanders-and-larry-david/.

16. Prokop, Andrew. "Read Bernie Sanders's Speech on Democratic Socialism in the United States." *Vox*. Last modified November 19, 2015. https://www .vox.com/2015/11/19/9762028/bernie-sanders-democratic-socialism.

17. Tumulty, Karen. "How Sanders caught fire in Iowa and turned the Clinton coronation into a real race." *Washington Post*. Last modified February 2, 2016. https://www.washingtonpost.com/politics/how-sanders-caught-fire-in -iowa-and-turned-the-clinton-coronation-into-a-real-race/2016/02/02 /83b08d22-c79a-11e5-8965-0607e0e265ce_story.html?utm_term =.7f6520a9634d.

18. Ibid.

19. Benen, Steve. "Sanders Makes History with New Hampshire Landslide." MSNBC. Last modified February 10, 2016. http://www.msnbc.com/rachel -maddow-show/sanders-makes-history-new-hampshire-landslide.

20. Langer, Gary, Gregory Holyk, and Chad Kiewiet De Jonge. "Black Voters Boost Hillary Clinton to South Carolina Primary Win." *ABC News*. Last modified February 29, 2016. https://abcnews.go.com/Politics/live-south -carolina-democratic-primary-exit-poll-analysis/story?id=37241467.

21. "Super Tuesday Results 2016." *New York Times*. Last modified September 29, 2016. https://www.nytimes.com/elections/2016/results/2016-03-01.

22. "March 15 Primary Results 2016."*New York Times*. Last modified September 29, 2016. https://www.nytimes.com/elections/2016/results/2016 -03-15.

23. Tobias, Manuela, and Nolan D. Mccaskill. "Bernie Sanders Wins Michigan in Stunning Upset." *Politico*. Last modified March 8, 2016. https://www .politico.com/story/2016/03/politico-breaking-news-sanders-wins -michigan-220460.

24. Wikipedia. "2016 Democratic Party Presidential Primaries." Wikipedia, the Free Encyclopedia. Last modified November 14, 2012. https://en.wikipedia .org/wiki/2016_Democratic_Party_presidential_primaries.

25. "Highlights from the Democratic Debate." *NYTimes.com*–Video. Accessed April 11, 2019. https://www.nytimes.com/video/us/politics/100000004328756 /highlights-from-the-democratic-debate.html.

26. Andrews, Wilson. "How Every New York City Neighborhood Voted in the Democratic Primary." *New York Times*. Last modified June 5, 2017. https:// www.nytimes.com/interactive/2016/04/19/us/elections/new-york-city -democratic-primary-results.html#11/40.7100/-73.9800.

27. Jacobs, Ben. "Bernie Sanders Pulls off Shock Victory over Hillary Clinton in Indiana." *The Guardian*. Last modified July 14, 2017. https://www .theguardian.com/us-news/2016/may/03/bernie-sanders-wins-indiana -democratic-primary.

28. Healy, Patrick, and Jonathan Martin. "After Victory in California, Hillary Clinton Turns toward Donald Trump." *New York Times*. Last modified January 20, 2018. https://www.nytimes.com/2016/06/08/us/politics/hillary -clinton-bernie-sanders-primary.html.

29. Wikipedia. "2016 California Democratic Primary." Wikipedia, the Free Encyclopedia. Last modified March 29, 2016. https://en.wikipedia.org/wiki /2016_California_Democratic_primary.

30. Nakashima, Ellen. "Russian government hackers penetrated DNC, stole opposition research on Trump." *Washington Post*. Last modified June 14, 2016. https://www.washingtonpost.com/world/national-security/russian -government-hackers-penetrated-dnc-stole-opposition-research-on-trump /2016/06/14/cf006cb4-316e-11e6-8ff7-7b6c1998b7a0_story.html.

31. Brazile, Donna. "Inside Hillary Clinton's Secret Takeover of the DNC." *Politico*. Last modified November 2, 2017. https://www.politico.com /magazine/story/2017/11/02/clinton-brazile-hacks-2016-215774.

32. Sanders, Bernie. "Bernie Sanders—National Live Stream Address." YouTube. Last modified June 16, 2016. https://www.youtube.com/watch?v=RzHSNjctOCk.

33. Lippmann, Daniel. "Ex-Clinton Staffers Slam Sanders over Private Jet Flights." *Politico*. Last modified February 25, 2019. https://www.politico.com/story/2019/02/25/bernie-sanders-hillary-clinton-private-jet-flights-1182793.

34. Gautney, Heather. "How Bernie Sanders Delivered the Most Progressive Platform in Democratic Party History." *The Nation*. Last modified July 12, 2016. https://www.thenation.com/article/how-bernie-sanders-delivered-the-most-progressive-platform-in-democratic-party-history/.

35. Haltiwanger, John. "Bernie Sanders Says Fellow 2020 Democratic Candidates Are Now Running on His 2016 Ideas That Were Originally Dismissed as 'too radical.'" *Business Insider*. Last modified March 8, 2019. https://www.businessinsider.com/bernie-sanders-democrats-running-on-my-2016-ideas-they-called-radical-2019-3.

36. Lutz, Eric. "Bernie Sanders, the Original Lefty Radical, Faces an Army of Mini-Mes." *The Hive*. Last modified February 19, 2019. https://www.vanityfair.com/news/2019/02/bernie-sanders-running-for-president-2020.

37. Kenton, Will. "Mixed Economic System." Investopedia. Last modified February 28, 2010. https://www.investopedia.com/terms/m/mixed-economic-system.asp.

38. Tokars, Mike. "Was Eisenhower More of a Socialist than Bernie Sanders?" *The Christian Science Monitor*. Last modified November 15, 2015. https://www.csmonitor.com/USA/Politics/2015/1115/Was-Eisenhower-more-of-a-socialist-than-Bernie-Sanders.

39. Sanders, Bernie. "Agenda for America: 12 Steps Forward." Sen. Bernie Sanders. Accessed April 8, 2019. https://www.sanders.senate.gov/agenda/.

CAMPAIGN PLATFORM

1. "Twitter Post." Welcome to Twitter. Accessed April 8, 2019. https://twitter.com/chrislhayes/status/1110695059190697990.

2. Greenberg, Jon. "Medicare for All: What It Is, and Isn't." *PolitiFact*. Accessed April 8, 2019.https://www.politifact.com/truth-o-meter/article/2019/feb/19/explaining-medicare-all/.

3. Kliff, Sarah. "Private Health Insurance Exists in Europe and Canada. Here's How It Works." *Vox*. Last modified February 12, 2019. https://www

.vox.com/health-care/2019/2/12/18215430/single-payer-private-health
-insurance-harris-sanders.

4. Pramuk, Jacob. "Bernie Sanders introduces new 'Medicare for All' bill as he
tries to set 2020 health-care agenda". CNBC. Last modified April 10, 2019.
https://www.cnbc.com/2019/04/10/bernie-sanders-unveils-medicare-for-all
-bill-amid-2020-democratic-primary.html.

5. Sanders, Bernie. "Financing Medicare for All." Sen. Bernie Sanders. Accessed
April 10, 2019. https://www.sanders.senate.gov/download/medicare-for-all
-2019-financing.

6. Sanders, Bernie. "The Medicare for All Act of 2019. Summary." Sen. Bernie
Sanders. Accessed April 10, 2019. https://www.sanders.senate.gov/download
/medicare-for-all-2019-summary.

7. "Sanders and Clyburn Introduce Bill to Expand Community Health
Centers." Sen. Bernie Sanders. Last modified March 28, 2019. https://www
.sanders.senate.gov/newsroom/press-releases/-sanders-and-clyburn
-introduce-bill-to-expand-community-health-centers.

8. Sanders, Bernie "Community Health Centers Act Summary." Senator
Bernie Sanders. Accessed April 9, 2019. https://www.sanders.senate.gov
/download/community-health-centers-act-summary?inline=file.

9. "Sen. Bernie Sanders and Rep. James Clyburn Introduce Bill to Expand Community Health Centers." Sen. Bernie Sanders. Accessed April 8, 2019. https://
www.sanders.senate.gov/newsroom/video-audio/sen-bernie-sanders-and-rep
-james-clyburn-introduce-bill-to-expand-community-health-centers.

10. "Sanders Joins Senate Leaders to Unveil $1 Trillion Infrastructure Plan."
Sen. Bernie Sanders. Last modified January 24, 2017. https://www.sanders
.senate.gov/newsroom/press-releases/-sanders-joins-senate-leaders-to-unveil
-1-trillion-infrastructure-plan.

11. Ibid.

12. "Sanders, Boxer Propose Climate Change Bills." Sen. Bernie Sanders. Last
modified February 14, 2013. https://www.sanders.senate.gov/newsroom
/press-releases/sanders-boxer-propose-climate-change-bills.

13. Sobczyk, Nick. "CLIMATE: Sanders Plots Green New Deal-style Bill."
E&E News. Last modified April 8, 2019. https://www.eenews.net/stories
/1060108433.

14. Rosanne, Olivia. "Bernie Sanders Enters 2020 Race, Promises Own Version
of Green New Deal." *Eco Watch*. Last modified March 22, 2019. https://
www.ecowatch.com/bernie-sanders-2020-2629410846.html.

15. "Pocan and Sanders Lead Democrats in Introducing Workplace Democracy Act." Congressman Mark Pocan. Last modified May 9, 2018. https://pocan .house.gov/media-center/press-releases/pocan-and-sanders-lead-democrats-in -introducing-workplace-democracy-act.

16. "Top Democrats Introduce Bill Raising Minimum Wage to $15." Sen. Bernie Sanders. Last modified January 16, 2019. https://www.sanders.senate .gov/newsroom/press-releases/top-democrats-introduce-bill-raising-minimum -wage-to-15.

17. "Sanders, Khanna Introduce the Stop WALMART Act to Put Workers over Shareholders." Sen. Bernie Sanders. Last modified November 15, 2018. https://www.sanders.senate.gov/newsroom/press-releases/sanders-khanna -introduce-the-stop-walmart-act-to-put-workers-over-shareholders.

18. "The Stop WALMART Act." Sen. Bernie Sanders. Accessed April 8, 2019. https://www.sanders.senate.gov/download/stop-walmart-act-summary.

19. "Twitter Post." Welcome to Twitter. Accessed April 8, 2019. https://twitter .com/SenSanders/status/1063084176440729600.

20. Ember, Sydney, and Jonathan Martin. "Bernie Sanders Apologizes Again to Women Who Were Mistreated in 2016 Campaign." *New York Times*. Last modified January 11, 2019. https://www.nytimes.com/2019/01/10/us /politics/sanders-sexism-apology.html.

21. Thompson, Alex. "Top Bernie Sanders 2016 Adviser Accused of Forcibly Kissing Subordinate." *Politico*. Last modified January 9, 2019. https://www .politico.com/story/2019/01/09/bernie-sanders-2016-robert-becker-women -inappropriate-behavior-1093836.

22. "Twitter Post." To the women on my 2016 campaign who were harassed or mistreated, thank you, from the bottom of my heart, for speaking out. I apologize. Last modified January 10, 2019. https://twitter.com/BernieSanders /status/1083425779407572992.

23. Ember, Sydney, and Katie Benner. "Sexism Claims From Bernie Sanders's 2016 Run: Paid Less, Treated Worse." *New York Times*. Last modified January 5, 2019. https://www.nytimes.com/2019/01/02/us/politics/bernie -sanders-campaign-sexism.html.

24. Ackerman, Seth, Matt Karp, Liza Featherstone, and Matthew Yglesias. "Don't Call It a Comeback." *Jacobin*. Accessed April 8, 2019. https://www .jacobinmag.com/2019/02/dont-call-it-a-comeback.

25. Summers, Juana. "Key Sanders 2016 Strategists Won't Return for 2020 Campaign." *Real Clear Politics*. Last modified February 27, 2019. https://

www.realclearpolitics.com/articles/2019/02/27/key_sanders_2016
_strategists_wont_return_for_2020_campaign_139600.html.

26. Seitz-Wald, Alex. "Bernie Sanders Staff Shake-up: Top Strategists Leave His Presidential Campaign." *NBC News*. Last modified February 26, 2019. https://www.nbcnews.com/politics/2020-election/bernie-sanders-staff -shakeup-top-strategists-leave-his-presidential-campaign-n976221.

27. "ALL In With Chris Hayes". December 12, 2016. TV program. MSNBC.

28. "Sanders Statement on Trump Tariffs." Sen. Bernie Sanders. Last modified June 1, 2018. https://www.sanders.senate.gov/newsroom/press-releases /sanders-statement-on-trump-tariffs.

29. Rogers, David. "POLITICO Analysis: At $2.3 Trillion Cost, Trump Tax Cuts Leave Big Gap." *Politico*. Last modified February 28, 2018. https:// www.politico.com/story/2018/02/28/tax-cuts-trump-gop-analysis-430781.

30. Tankersley, Jim. "It's Official: The Trump Tax Cuts Didn't Pay for Them-selves in Year One." *New York Times*. Last modified January 12, 2019. https:// www.nytimes.com/2019/01/11/business/trump-tax-cuts-revenue.html.

31. "Adding Up Senator Sanders's Campaign Proposals So Far." Committee for a Responsible Federal Budget. Last modified February 23, 2018. http:// www.crfb.org/papers/adding-senator-sanderss-campaign-proposals-so-far.

32. Stein, Jeff. "Bernie Sanders's 2020 policy agenda: Medicare for All; action on climate change; $15-an-hour minimum wage." *Washington Post*. n.d. https:// www.washingtonpost.com/us-policy/2019/02/19/bernie-sanderss-policy -agenda-medicare-all-action-climate-change-an-hour-minimum-wage/.

33. Kelton, Stephanie, Scott Fullwiler, Catherine Ruetschlin, and Marshall Stein Baum. "The Macroeconomic Effects of Student Debt Cancellation." The Sanders Institute. Accessed April 8, 2019. https://www.sandersinstitute .com/blog/the-macroeconomic-effects-of-student-debt-cancellation.

34. "The Sanders Institute announced it was ceasing operations on March 15, 2019 and closing its doors by May 2019 to avoid any appearance of affiliation with the senator's presidential campaign. (Source: AP) Peoples, Steve, and Stephen Braun. "Institute Founded by Sanders's Wife, Son is Shutting Down." AP News. Last modified March 15, 2019. https://www .apnews.com/9e4794da89ab448399f3ff1457464d1b.

35. Stein, Jeff. "Bernie Sanders's 2020 policy agenda: Medicare for All; action on climate change; $15-an-hour minimum wage." *Washington Post*. Last Modified February 19, 2019. https://www.washingtonpost.com/us-policy

/2019/02/19/bernie-sanderss-policy-agenda-medicare-all-action-climate
-change-an-hour-minimum-wage/.

36. Blake, Aaron. "More young people voted for Bernie Sanders than Trump
and Clinton combined." *Washington Post*. June 20, 2016 https://www
.washingtonpost.com/news/the-fix/wp/2016/06/20/more-young-people
-voted-for-bernie-sanders-than-trump-and-clinton-combined-by-a-lot/.

37. Sanders, Linley. "The Youth Vote Had a Big Impact on the 2018 Midterms,
but It Could've Been MUCH Bigger." *Teen Vogue*. Last modified November
10, 2018. https://www.teenvogue.com/story/2018-midterms-youth-voter
-turnout-still-room-for-growth.

38. Varathan, Preeti. "The Number of U.S. Banks That Are 'Too Big to Fail'
Just Shrank." *Quartz*. Last modified May 23, 2018. https://qz.com/1286289
/dodd-frank-act-explained-the-number-of-too-big-to-fail-banks-just-shrank/.

39. Sanders, Bernie "Sanders, Sherman Introduce Legislation to Break Up Too
Big to Fail Financial Institutions." Sen. Bernie Sanders. Last modified
October 3, 2018. https://www.sanders.senate.gov/newsroom/press-releases
/sanders-sherman-introduce-legislation-to-break-up-too-big-to-fail-financial
-institutions.

40. Sanders, Bernie. "Sanders, Sherman Introduce Legislation to Break Up Too
Big to Fail Financial Institutions." Sen. Bernie Sanders. Last modified
October 3, 2018. https://www.sanders.senate.gov/newsroom/press-releases
/sanders-sherman-introduce-legislation-to-break-up-too-big-to-fail-financial
-institutions.

41. Paletta, Darmian. "McConnell calls deficit 'very disturbing,' blames federal
spending, Dismisses criticism of tax cut." *Washington Post*. Last Modified
October 16, 2018. https://www.washingtonpost.com/business/economy
/mcconnell-calls-deficit-very-disturbing-blames-federal-spending-dismisses
-criticism-of-tax-cut/2018/10/16/a5b93da0-d15c-11e8-8c22-fa2ef74bd6d6
_story.html.

42. Sanders, Bernie "Sanders, DeFazio Introduce Bill to Expand Social
Security." Sen. Bernie Sanders. Last modified February 13, 2019. https://
www.sanders.senate.gov/newsroom/press-releases/sanders-defazio-introduce
-bill-to-expand-social-security.

43. Sanders, Bernie "Sanders Introduces Estate Tax Reform to Combat
Inequality." Sen. Bernie Sanders. Last Modified January 31, 2019. https://
www.sanders.senate.gov/newsroom/press-releases/sanders-introduces-estate
-tax-reform-to-combat-inequality.

44. Sanders, Bernie "Sanders Introduces Estate Tax Reform to Combat Inequality." Sen. Bernie Sanders. Last Modified January 31, 2019. https://www.sanders.senate.gov/newsroom/press-releases/sanders-introduces-estate-tax-reform-to-combat-inequality.

45. CBS NEWS. "Bernie Sanders Announces 2020 Run: Full Transcript." Last modified February 19, 2019. https://www.cbsnews.com/news/bernie-sanders-2020-running-for-president-announcement-full-transcript-today-2019-02-19/.

46. Gibson, Ginger. "U.S. Senator Bernie Sanders against Increasing Number of Supreme Court Justices." Reuters. Last modified April 2, 2019. https://www.reuters.com/article/us-usa-election-sanders/us-senator-bernie-sanders-against-increasing-number-of-supreme-court-justices-idUSKCN1RD3AL.

47. Fineout, Gary, and Marc A. Caputo. "As 2020 Nears, Puerto Rico Statehood Looms Large in Florida." *Politico*. Last modified April 4, 2019. https://www.politico.com/states/florida/story/2019/04/04/as-2020-nears-puerto-rico-statehood-looms-large-in-florida-951370.

48. Zhou, Li. "Bernie Sanders Declines to Back Reparations." *Vox*. Last modified March 1, 2019. https://www.vox.com/policy-and-politics/2019/3/1/18246394/bernie-sanders-reparations-slavery-2020-harris-booker-warren.

49. Walker, Hunter. "Bernie Sanders Says 'there should be a Study' on Slavery Reparations." Yahoo News. Last modified April 5, 2019. https://news.yahoo.com/bernie-sanders-says-there-should-be-a-study-on-slavery-reparations-162826965.html.

50. Walker, Hunter. "Bernie Sanders Campaign Touts Its Diversity and Fights 'the Narrative of 2016'." Yahoo News. Last modified April 2, 2019. https://news.yahoo.com/bernie-sanders-campaign-touts-diversity-fights-narrative-2016-194035907.html.

51. Robertson, Derek. "Bernie Sanders Is Quietly Remaking the Democrats' Foreign Policy in His Own Image." *Politico*. Last modified October 17, 2018. https://www.politico.com/magazine/story/2018/10/17/bernie-sanders-is-quietly-remaking-the-democrats-foreign-policy-in-his-own-image-221313.

52. Ward, Alex. "Senate Passes Resolution to End U.S. Role in Yemen War." *Vox*. Last modified March 13, 2019. https://www.vox.com/2019/3/13/18263894/yemen-war-senate-sanders-murphy-lee.

53. Congress.gov. "S.J.Res.7 - 116th Congress (2019-2020): A Joint Resolution to Direct the Removal of United States Armed Forces from Hostilities in the Republic of Yemen That Have Not Been Authorized by Congress."

Library of Congress. Last modified April 4, 2019. https://www.congress.gov/bill/116th-congress/senate-joint-resolution/7/.

54. Congress.gov. "Actions–S.J.Res.54–115th Congress (2017–2018): A Joint Resolution to Direct the Removal of United States Armed Forces from Hostilities in the Republic of Yemen That Have Not Been Authorized by Congress." Library of Congress. Last modified December 19, 2018. https://www.congress.gov/bill/115th-congress/senate-joint-resolution/54/all-actions.

55. *USA Today*. "Sanders & Lee: Congress Just Told Trump to Get U.S. Troops out of Yemen. Next, Afghanistan?" *USA Today*. Last modified April 4, 2019. https://www.usatoday.com/story/opinion/2019/04/04/congress-yemen-war-powers-bernie-sanders-mike-lee-column/3363199002/.

56. Ward, Alex. "Read: Bernie Sanders's Big Foreign Policy Speech." *Vox*. Last modified September 21, 2017. https://www.vox.com/world/2017/9/21/16345600/bernie-sanders-full-text-transcript-foreign-policy-speech-westminster.

57. Klion, David. "Why Don't Sanders Supporters Care About the Russia Investigation?" *New York Times*. Last modified January 20, 2018. https://www.nytimes.com/2017/11/14/opinion/bernie-supporters-russia-investigation.html.

58. Ward, Alex. "Read: Bernie Sanders's Big Foreign Policy Speech." *Vox*. Last modified September 21, 2017. https://www.vox.com/world/2017/9/21/16345600/bernie-sanders-full-text-transcript-foreign-policy-speech-westminster.

59. "Sanders Speech at SAIS: Building A Global Democratic Movement to Counter Authoritarianism." Sen. Bernie Sanders. Last modified October 9, 2018. https://www.sanders.senate.gov/newsroom/press-releases/sanders-speech-at-sais-building-a-global-democratic-movement-to-counter-authoritarianism.

60. Apper, Megan, and Ilan Ben-Meir. "Sanders In 1985: Sandinista Leader 'Impressive'? Castro 'Totally Transformed' Cuba." *BuzzFeed News*. Last modified June 25, 2015. https://www.buzzfeednews.com/article/meganapper/sanders-in-1985-sandinista-leader-impressive-castro-totally.

61. Partlow, Joshua. "From rebel to strongman: How Daniel Ortega became the thing he fought against." *Washington Post*. Accessed August 24, 2018. https://www.washingtonpost.com/world/the_americas/from-rebel-to-strongman-how-daniel-ortega-became-the-thing-he-fought-against/2018/08/24/117d000a-97fe-11e8-818b-e9b7348cd87d_story.html.

62. Walters, Jonah. "Ortega's Betrayal." *Jacobin*. Accessed April 8, 2019. https://www.jacobinmag.com/2016/04/bernie-sanders-sandinistas-daniel-orega-nicaraguan-revolution/.

63. Catholics 4 Bernie "Bernie Sanders: Nicaragua Interview (8/8/1985)." YouTube. Last modified July 21, 2015. https://youtu.be/_6liJbu9ZCY.

64. "Sanders in Delegation Traveling to Cuba." Sen. Bernie Sanders. Last modified February 6, 2014. https://www.sanders.senate.gov/newsroom/press-releases/sanders-in-delegation-traveling-to-cuba.

65. Congress.gov. "Cosponsors - S.299 - 114th Congress (2015-2016): Freedom to Travel to Cuba Act of 2015." Library of Congress. Last modified January 29, 2015. https://www.congress.gov/bill/114th-congress/senate-bill/299/cosponsors.

66. Ibid.

67. Goldberg, Jeffrey. "Fidel: 'Cuban Model Doesn't Even Work for Us Anymore'." *The Atlantic*. Last modified September 8, 2010. https://www.theatlantic.com/international/archive/2010/09/fidel-cuban-model-doesnt-even-work-for-us-anymore/62602/.

68. Team Fix. "Transcript: The Post-Univision Democratic debate, annotated." *Washington Post*. Last modified March 9, 2016. https://www.washingtonpost.com/news/the-fix/wp/2016/03/09/transcript-the-post-univision-democratic-debate-annotated/.

69. Sakuma, Amanda. "Cuban, Venezuelan Immigrants Wrestle with Bernie Sanders's Brand of Socialism." MSNBC. Last modified March 14, 2016. http://www.msnbc.com/msnbc/cuban-venezuelan-immigrants-wrestle-bernie-sanders-brand-socialism.

70. Gupta, Girish, and Corina Pons. "Venezuela's Maduro Rooting for 'revolutionary Friend' Sanders in U.S. Campaign" Reuters. Last modified June 1, 2016. https://www.reuters.com/article/us-venezuela-usa-idUSKCN0YN32Q.

71. "Close The Gaps: Disparities That Threaten America." Sen. Bernie Sanders. Last modified August 5, 2011. https://www.sanders.senate.gov/newsroom/must-read/close-the-gaps-disparities-that-threaten-america.

72. Roberts, Dan. "Bernie Sanders Rejects 'vicious' Attack over His Support for UK Labour Leader." *The Guardian*. Last modified July 14, 2017. https://www.theguardian.com/us-news/2015/sep/15/bernie-sanders-clinton-super-pac-jeremy-corbyn.

73. CNN Live Event/Special. "CNN Town hall with Sen. Bernie Sanders, 2020 Presidential Campaign Candidate". February 25, 2019.

74. OAS. "OAS Permanent Council Agrees "to Not Recognize the Legitimacy of Nicolas Maduro's New Term"." OAS–Organization of American States: Democracy for Peace, Security, and Development. Last modified August 1, 2009. http://www.oas.org/en/media_center/press_release.asp?sCodigo=E -001/19.

75. "Recognition of Juan Guaido as Venezuela's Interim President by Several European Countries." U.S. Department of State. Last modified February 28, 2019. https://www.state.gov/secretary/remarks/2019/02/288744.htm.

76. OAS. "OAS Member States Issue Joint Statement on Venezuela." U.S. Mission to the Organization of American States. Last modified January 24, 2019. https://usoas.usmission.gov/oas-member-states-issue-joint-statement -on-venezuela/.

77. Caputo, Marc. "'He is Not Going to Be the Nominee': Dems Slam Sanders over Maduro Stance." *Politico*. Last modified February 21, 2019. https:// www.politico.com/story/2019/02/21/bernie-sanders-venezuela-maduro -1179636.

78. Watson, Michael. "The Democratic Socialists of America Back Strongman Maduro." Capital Research Center. Last modified January 25, 2019. https:// capitalresearch.org/article/the-democratic-socialists-of-americas-corrupt -car-wash/.

79. Sirota, David. "Hugo Chavez's Economic Miracle." *Salon Magazine*. Last modified March 6, 2013. https://www.salon.com/2013/03/06/hugo_chavezs _economic_miracle/.

80. Simonson, Joseph. "Bernie's New Speechwriter Applauded 'Chavez's Economic Miracle.'" *Washington Examiner*. Last modified March 19, 2019. https://www.washingtonexaminer.com/news/bernies-new-speechwriter -applauded-chavezs-economic-miracle.

81. Erlanger, Steven. "Bernie Sanders's Kibbutz Found. Surprise: It's Socialist." *New York Times*. Last modified December 21, 2017. https://www.nytimes .com/2016/02/06/us/politics/bernie-sanders-kibbutz.html.

82. Beauchamp, Zack. "Bernie Sanders Just Shattered an American Taboo on Israel." *Vox*. Last modified April 15, 2016. https://www.vox.com/2016/4/15 /11437832/bernie-sanders-just-shattered-an-american-taboo-on-israel.

83. Cortellessa, Eric. "Where Does Bernie Sanders Stand on Israel?" *The Times of Israel*. Last modified February 1, 2016. https://www.timesofisrael.com /where-does-bernie-sanders-stand-on-israel-2/.

84. Tibon, Amir. "Sanders' 2020 Run Assures Israel Central Spot in Campaign." *Haaretz*. Last modified February 20, 2019. https://www.haaretz .com/us-news/premium-sanders-2020-run-assures-israel-central-spot-in -campaign-1.6955171.

85. Samuels, Brett. "Senate Dems Urge Trump to Remain in Iran Deal Ahead of Announcement." *The Hill*. Last modified May 7, 2018. https://thehill .com/homenews/senate/386604-senate-dems-urge-trump-to-remain-in -iran-deal-ahead-of-announcement.

86. Kumar Sen., Ashish. "Strange Bedfellows: Saudi Arabia, Israel Oppose Iran Nuclear Deal for Different Reasons." Atlantic Council. Accessed April 8, 2019. https://www.atlanticcouncil.org/blogs/new-atlanticist/strange-bedfellows -saudi-arabia-israel-oppose-iran-nuclear-deal-for-different-reasons.

87. Sanders, Bernie "Sanders Statement on Anti-BDS Bill." Sen. Bernie Sanders. Last modified January 28, 2019. https://www.sanders.senate.gov /newsroom/press-releases/sanders-statement-on-anti-bds-bill.

88. Axelrod, Tal. "Sanders Defends Omar: Can't Equate Anti-Semitism with 'legitimate Criticism' of Israel." *The Hill*. Last modified March 6, 2019. https://thehill.com/homenews/senate/432926-sanders-on-omar-cant-equate -anti-semitism-with-legitimate-criticism-of.

89. Uhrmacher, Kevin, Kevin Schaul, Paulina Firozi, and Jeff Stein. "Medicare-for-all: Where Democrats stand on health-care issues." *Washington Post*. Last modified April 9, 2019. Last Accessed April 10, 2019. https://www .washingtonpost.com/graphics/politics/policy-2020/medicare-for-all/.

BACKGROUND AND EDUCATION

1. "Generations and Age." Pew Research Center. Last modified February 26, 2019. https://www.pewresearch.org/topics/generations-and-age/.

2. Prokop, Andrew. "Bernie Sanders's Brother Gave a Tearful Tribute to Bernie and Their Parents at the DNC." *Vox*. Last modified July 26, 2016. https:// www.vox.com/2016/7/26/12290578/bernie-sanders-brother-larry-dnchttps: //www.vox.com/2016/7/26/12290578/bernie-sanders-brother-larry-dnc.

3. Ibid.

4. Newell, Jim. "Can Bernie Sanders Finally Start Acting Like the One Thing He's Never Been: The Favorite?" *Slate Magazine*. Accessed April 8, 2019. https://slate.com/news-and-politics/2019/04/bernie-sanders-2020 -presidential-race.html.

5. Bump, Philip. "The untold story of Bernie Sanders, high school track star." *Washington Post*. Last modified January 29, 2016. https://www.washingtonpost.com/news/the-fix/wp/2016/01/29/the-untold-story-of-bernie-sanders-high-school-track-star/?utm_term=.0e2ba22493aa.

6. Ibid.

7. CNN Library. "Bernie Sanders Fast Facts." CNN. Last modified March 6, 2019. https://www.cnn.com/2015/05/27/us/bernie-sanders-fast-facts/index.html.

8. Felsenthal, Carol. "Bernie Sanders Found Socialism at the University of Chicago." *Chicago Magazine*. Accessed April 8, 2019. https://www.chicagomag.com/Chicago-Magazine/Felsenthal-Files/May-2015/Bernie-Sanders-University-of-Chicago/.

9. Stern, Grant. "Fact-Check: Bernie Sanders Has Been A Warrior For Civil Rights His ENTIRE Life." *Occupy Democrats*. Last modified August 17, 2016. http://occupydemocrats.com/2016/02/17/fact-check-bernie-sanders-has-been-a-warrior-for-civil-rights-his-entire-life/.

10. Pearce, Matt. "When Martin Luther King Jr. Took His Fight into the North, and Saw a New Level of Hatred." *Los Angeles Times*. Last modified January 18, 2016. http://www.latimes.com/nation/la-na-mlk-chicago-20160118-story.html.

11. Kruse, Michael. "Bernie Sanders Has a Secret." *Politico*. Last modified July 9, 2015. https://www.politico.com/magazine/story/2015/07/bernie-sanders-vermont-119927.

12. Murphy, Tim. "Read Bernie Sanders's 1970s-era Essays on Sex, Cancer, Revolution, and Fluoride." *Mother Jones*. Last modified February 19, 2019. https://www.motherjones.com/politics/2015/07/bernie-sanders-vermont-freeman-sexual-freedom-fluoride/.

13. Harvard Kennedy School. "Bernard Sanders." The Institute of Politics at Harvard University. Accessed April 8, 2019. https://iop.harvard.edu/fellows/bernard-sanders.

14. Multiple-Authors "Liberty Union Party." Wikipedia, the Free Encyclopedia. Accessed April 8, 2019. https://en.wikipedia.org/wiki/Liberty_Union_Party.

15. Ibid.

16. Knight, Michael. "Vermont Socialist Plans Mayoralty with Bias toward Poor." *The New York Times*. Last modified March 8, 1981. https://www.nytimes.com/1981/03/08/us/vermont-socialist-plans-mayoralty-with-bias-toward-poor.html.

17. Margolis, Jon. "Bernie of Burlington." *New Republic*. Last modified March 14, 1983. https://newrepublic.com/article/122285/bernie-burlington.

18. "Just Jane: Activist Roots Pull Sanders Home to Goddard College." *Burlington Free Press*; August 31, 1996. Accessed April 9, 2019 via Wikipedia.

19. Solsbak, Kayla. "Bernie Sanders's Stepchildren Are Leaders, Too." *Bustle*. Last modified February 4, 2016. https://www.bustle.com/articles/139648 -who-are-bernie-sanders-stepchildren-the-vermont-senator-usually-stays -mum-about-his-family.

20. Ibid.

21. McCarthy, Colman. "A Marriage of Ideas and Service." *Washington Post*. Last modified December 3, 1996. https://www.washingtonpost.com/archive /sports/1996/12/03/a-marriage-of-ideas-and-service/e929aec1-8cde-45af-9c9a -83c2319ea801/.

22. Landers, Elizabeth. "Adviser Says Bernie Sanders's Wife Cleared in College Land Deal Investigation." CNN. Last modified November 13, 2018. https://www.cnn.com/2018/11/13/politics/jane-sanders-burlington-college /index.html.

FROM MAYOR TO REPRESENTATIVE

1. Qiu, Linda. "Bernie Sanders Was the Roll Call Amendment King from 1995 to 2007." *PolitiFact*. Last modified February 13, 2016. https://www .politifact.com/truth-o-meter/statements/2016/mar/24/bernie-s/bernie -sanders-was-roll-call-amendment-king-1995-2/.

2. Cabaniss, Will. "George Will Describes Bernie Sanders's Soviet Union Honeymoon." *PolitiFact*. Last modified August 12, 2015. https://www .politifact.com/punditfact/statements/2015/aug/12/george-will/george-will -reminds-readers-about-bernie-sanders-u/.

3. "Electoral History of Bernie Sanders." Wikipedia, the Free Encyclopedia. Accessed April 8, 2019. https://en.wikipedia.org/wiki/Electoral_history_of _Bernie_Sanders.

4. CNN Library. "Bernie Sanders Fast Facts." CNN. Last modified March 6, 2019. https://www.cnn.com/2015/05/27/us/bernie-sanders-fast-facts/index.html.

5. Kolbert, Elizabeth. "Political Outsider Coping With Life as an Insider." *New York Times*. Last modified August 18, 1991. https://www.nytimes .com/1991/08/18/us/political-outsider-coping-with-life-as-an-insider.html.

6. Daly, Christopher B. "Or Vermont's Sanders, Victory followed long Path." *Washington Post*. Last modified November 11, 1990. https://www
.washingtonpost.com/archive/politics/1990/11/11/for-vermonts-sanders
-victory-followed-long-path/36a3036c-d738-4039-a728-891ae9aba9f5/
?utm_term=.045718cf3dbf.

7. Ibid.

8. Sanders, Bernie. "*Outsider in the House*." Brooklyn: Verso, 1997.

9. Bernstein, Jared, and John Schmitt. "Making Work Pay: The Impact of the 1996–97 Minimum Wage Increase." Economic Policy Institute. Accessed April 8, 2019. https://www.epi.org/publication/studies_stmwp/.

10. Ibid.

11. Multiple-Authors. "Northeast Interstate Dairy Compact." Wikipedia, the Free Encyclopedia. Accessed April 8, 2019. https://en.wikipedia.org/wiki
/Northeast_Interstate_Dairy_Compact.

12. CDC. "About NPCR | Cancer | CDC." Centers for Disease Control and Prevention. Last modified March 14, 2019. https://www.cdc.gov/cancer
/npcr/about.htm.

13. "As Progressive Caucus Satisfied On EITC Provision". August 2, 1993. *National Journal's Congress Daily*. UPI (Accessed 4/6/2019 Nexis.com).

14. "Progressives offer Contract option". January 18, 1995. UPI. (Accessed 4/6/2019 Nexis.com).

15. Bleifuss, Joel. "Whose Party Is It? A progressive runs on the issues". February 3, 1997. *In These Times*. (Accessed 4/6/2019 Nexis.com).

16. Shields, Janice C. "Strange Bedfellows." May 12, 1997. *In These Times*. (Accessed 4/6/2019 Nexis.com).

17. Ibid.

18. Thirty-one of Rep. Sanders's amendments passed with unanimous consent.

19. Sanders, Bernie "Legislative Landmarks." Sen. Bernie Sanders. Accessed April 8, 2019. https://www.sanders.senate.gov/legislative-landmarks.

20. H.Amdt.255—108th Congress (2003–2004)

21. H.Amdt.404—107th Congress (2001–2002)

22. H.R.7—102nd Congress (1991–1992)

23. H.R.1025—103rd Congress (1993–1994), House Vote #614

24. H.J.Res.77—102nd Congress (1991–1992)

25. H.J.Res.64—107th Congress (2001–2002)

26. H.J.Res.114—107th Congress (2001–2002)

27. H.R.3450—103rd Congress (1993–1994)

28. H.R.2546—108th Congress (2003–2004)

29. H.R.2622—108th Congress (2003–2004)

30. Klein, Rick, and Globe Staff. "Party Shuns Vermont Democrats in Race." Local Boston Breaking News, Sports, Weather and Events | Boston.com. Last modified July 13, 2006. http://archive.boston.com/news/nation/articles /2006/07/13/party_shuns_vermont_democrats_in_race/.

31. "The impact of differences between consumer- and creditor-purchased credit scores Report to Congress." Consumer Financial Protection Bureau. Last modified July 19, 2011. https://files.consumerfinance.gov/f/2011/07 /Report_20110719_CreditScores.pdf.

32. Ring, Wilson. "Sanders, Welch Are Winners in Vermont." November 8, 2006. Associated Press. (Accessed 4/6/2019 Nexis.com).

SENATE CAREER

1. Ibid.

2. Ridgeway, James. "A Socialist in the Millionaires' Club: An Interview with Bernie Sanders." *Mother Jones.* Last modified June 27, 2017. https://www .motherjones.com/politics/2006/11/socialist-millionaires-club-interview -bernie-sanders/.

3. Jaffe, Greg, and Ed O'Keefe. "Obama accepts resignation of VA Secretary Shinseki." *Washington Post.* Last modified May 20, 2014. https://www .washingtonpost.com/politics/shinseki-apologizes-for-va-health-care -scandal/2014/05/30/e605885a-e7f0-11e3-8f90-73e071f3d637_story.html.

4. Stein, Sam. "Bernie Sanders, the Wide-Eyed Pragmatist." *Huff Post.* Last modified June 17, 2015. https://www.huffpost.com/entry/bernie-sanders -2016_n_7514328.

5. Stein, Sam. "Congressional Leaders Have Actually Agreed On A VA Reform Bill." *Huff Post.* Last modified August 28, 2014. https://www .huffpost.com/entry/va-reform-deal-unveiled_n_5627066.

6. Ibid.

7. H.R.3230—113th Congress (2013–2014)

8. Shane III, Leo. "Bernie Sanders's Senate Work at the Heart of VA's Latest Woes." *Military Times.* Last modified February 18, 2016. https://www .militarytimes.com/news/2016/02/18/bernie-sanders-senate-work-at-the -heart-of-va-s-latest-woes/.

9. Ibid.

10. S.1094—115th Congress (2017–2018)

11. Schilling, Joan. "Community Health Centers Continue to Help Underserved Areas." Michigan State University. *MSU Extension, Chronic Disease*. Last modified September 6, 2018. https://www.canr.msu.edu/news /community-health-centers-continue-to-help-underserved-areas.

12. Jacobson, Louis. "Bernie Sanders Exaggerates with Claim That He Helped Write Obamacare." *PolitiFact*. Last modified January 18, 2016. https:// www.politifact.com/truth-o-meter/statements/2016/jan/18/bernie-s/fact -checking-bernie-sanders-claim-he-helped-write/.

13. Fang, Lee. "GOP Officials Publicly Denounce Bernie Sanders' Obamacare Expansion, Quietly Request Funding." *The Intercept*. Last modified July 6, 2015. https://theintercept.com/2015/07/06/gop-senators-support-sanders -obamacare-expansion/.

14. Sanders, Bernie "Release: Sanders Wins Community Health Champion Award." Sen. Bernie Sanders. Last modified February 25, 2010. https:// www.sanders.senate.gov/newsroom/press-releases/release-sanders-wins -community-health-champion-award.

15. History.com Editors. "Great Recession." *History*. Last modified August 21, 2018. https://www.history.com/topics/21st-century/recession.

16. S. Amdt. 3738—111th Congress (2009–2010)

17. Congress.gov. "S.Amdt.3738 to S.Amdt.3739 to S.3217 - 111th Congress (2009–2010) - Actions." Congress.gov | Library of Congress. Last modified May 11, 2010. https://www.congress.gov/amendment/111th-congress/senate -amendment/3738/actions?r=426&s=a.

18. Sanders, Bernie "Sanders's Fed Transparency Amendment Passes." Sen. Bernie Sanders. Accessed April 9, 2019. https://www.sanders.senate.gov /newsroom/video-audio/sanders-fed-transparency-amendment-passes.

19. S.Amdt. 2276—111th Congress (2009–2010)

20. Gaudiano, Nicole. "Senate Democrats Tap Bernie Sanders to Lead Outreach." *USA Today*. Last modified November 16, 2016. https://www .usatoday.com/story/news/2016/11/16/senate-democrats-tap-bernie-sanders -lead-outreach/93960822/.

21. GovTrack.us. "Bernard Sanders's 2018 Legislative Statistics." GovTrack.us. Last modified January 20, 2019. https://www.govtrack.us/congress /members/bernard_sanders/400357/report-card/2018.

22. Weigel, David. "Sen. Bernie Sanders will seek the Democratic presidential nomination in 2020." *Washington Post*. Last modified February 19, 2019.

https://www.washingtonpost.com/powerpost/sen-bernie-sanders-will-seek
-the-democratic-presidential-nomination-in-2020/2019/02/19/be5b0216
-002e-11e9-862a-b6a6f3ce8199_story.html?utm_term=.a12cf766c0f9.

23. Kinzel, Bob. "He's In For 2020: Bernie Sanders Is Running For President Again." Vermont Public Radio. Last modified February 19, 2019. https://www .vpr.org/post/hes-2020-bernie-sanders-running-president-again#stream/0.

24. Ibid.

25. Summers, Juana, and Julie Pace. "Bernie Sanders is Adjusting to a New Campaign Role: Front-runner." *USA Today*. Last modified April 8, 2019. https://www.usatoday.com/story/news/politics/elections/2019/04/08 /bernie-sanders-adjusts-new-role-presidential-frontrunner/3400364002/.

ANALYSIS: SANDERS'S CHANCES FOR WINNING
THE NOMINATION AND PRESIDENCY

1. Real Clear politics. "Election 2020–2020 Democratic Presidential Nomination." *RealClearPolitics*. Accessed April 11, 2019. https://www .realclearpolitics.com/epolls/2020/president/us/2020_democratic _presidential_nomination-6730.html#polls.

2. Summers, Juana, and Julie Pace. "Bernie Sanders is Adjusting to a New Campaign Role: Front-runner." *USA Today*. Last modified April 8, 2019. https://www.usatoday.com/story/news/politics/elections/2019/04/08/bernie -sanders-adjusts-new-role-presidential-frontrunner/3400364002/.

3. Trende, Sean. "Evaluating the 2020 Democratic Primary Field." *RealClearPolitics*. Last modified April 9, 2019. https://www.realclearpolitics .com/articles/2019/04/09/evaluating_the_2020_democratic_primary_field _139997.html.

4. Alonso-Saldivar, Ricardo. "Poll: Support for 'Medicare-for-all' Fluctuates with Details." AP News. Last modified January 23, 2019. https://www .apnews.com/4516833e7fb644c9aa8bcc11048b2169.

5. Whitesides, John. "Bernie Sanders Gets Personal As He Hits the 2020 Campaign Trail." Reuters. Last modified March 2, 2019. https://www .reuters.com/article/us-usa-election-sanders/bernie-sanders-gets-personal -as-he-hits-the-2020-campaign-trail-idUSKCN1QJ095.

6. Sullivan, Sean. "At his presidential campaign kickoff, Sanders gets per-sonal." *Washington Post*. Last modified March 2, 2019. https://www .washingtonpost.com/politics/at-his-campaign-kickoff-bernie-sanders-will

-emphasize-his-personal-story/2019/03/02/1244c2e0-3cd9-11e9-aaae
-69364b2ed137_story.html?utm_term=.35978a9a4a84.

7. Real Clear Politics. "Election 2020–2020 Democratic Presidential Nomination." *RealClearPolitics* . Accessed April 11, 2019. https://www.realclearpolitics.com/epolls/2020/president/us/2020_democratic_presidential_nomination-6730.html#polls.

8. Hughes, Greg, and John King. "Elizabeth Warren's Polling Problem: Gaining Support from Next Door." CNN. Last modified March 4, 2019. https://www.cnn.com/2019/03/03/politics/inside-politics-forecast-march-3-cnntv/index.html?no-st=1553567090.

9. Real Clear Politics. "Election 2020—Iowa Democratic Presidential Caucus." *RealClearPolitics* . Accessed April 11, 2019. https://www.realclearpolitics.com/epolls/2020/president/ia/iowa_democratic_presidential_caucus-6731.html.

10. Kimball, Spencer. "South Carolina 2020 Poll: Biden Leads Primary Field by Wide Margin; President Trump Popular with Base." Emerson Polling Reportable News. Accessed April 11, 2019. https://emersonpolling.reportablenews.com/pr/south-carolina-2020-poll-biden-leads-primary-field-by-wide-margin-president-trump-popular-with-base.

11. Rodrigo, Chris M. "Sanders Leads Poll of Young Democrats by Double Digits." *The Hill*. Last modified April 1, 2019. https://thehill.com/homenews/campaign/436675-sanders-leads-poll-of-young-democratic-voters-by-double-digits.

12. Kimball, Spencer. "Wisconsin 2020: Bernie Sanders Leads Democratic Field; Trump Competitive in General Election." Emerson Polling Reportable News. Accessed April 11, 2019. https://emersonpolling.reportablenews.com/pr/wisconsin-2020-bernie-sanders-leads-democratic-field-trump-competitive-in-general-election.

13. Caputo, Marc A. "'He is Not Going to Be the Nominee': Dems Slam Sanders over Maduro Stance." *Politico*. Last modified February 21, 2019. https://www.politico.com/story/2019/02/21/bernie-sanders-venezuela-maduro-1179636.

14. Heintz, Paul. "Bernie Sanders to Run for President in 2020." Seven Days. Last modified February 19, 2019. https://www.sevendaysvt.com/OffMessage/archives/2019/02/19/bernie-sanders-to-run-for-president-in-2020.

15. Feloni, Richard. "Dismissing Bernie Sanders as a Communist Shows Your 'Profound Ignorance,' Says One of the Most Influential Behind-the-scenes Figures in American Business." *Business Insider*. Last modified February 28,

2019. https://www.businessinsider.com/delaware-chief-justice-leo-strine
-says-bernie-sanders-is-not-radical-2019-2.

16. Real Clear Politics. "Election 2020—General Election: Trump vs. Sanders."
RealClearPolitics . Accessed April 11, 2019. https://www.realclearpolitics.com
/epolls/2020/president/us/general_election_trump_vs_sanders-6250.html.

17. Allen, Jonathan. "Why the 2020 Democratic Primary Could Turn into
'Lord of the Flies.'" *NBC News*. Last modified January 24, 2019. https://
www.nbcnews.com/politics/2020-election/why-2020-democratic-primary
-could-turn-lord-flies-n961236.